**ALSO BY WILLIAM BAPTISTE
In the *HUMAN RIGHTS EDUCATION FOR LASTING FREE DEMOCRACY* Book Series:**

THE FOUNDATIONAL PRINCIPLES OF HUMAN RIGHTS AND DEMOCRACY
(Plus 10 Core Principles of Lasting Democracy)

KNIGHTS OF HUMAN RIGHTS, LADIES OF LASTING DEMOCRACY
Handbook Manifesto of the Global Solidarity Movement

DEMOCRACY 101
A Voter's and Politician's Manual for Lasting Democracy

PRO-LIFE EQUALS PRO-DEMOCRACY
A Sequel to Aleksandr Solzhenitsyn's *The Gulag Archipelago*

THE ANTI-COMMUNIST MANIFESTO

COMING SOON FROM WILLIAM BAPTISTE:

KILLING HUMANS IS WRONG

NO FRUIT WITHOUT ROOTS

THINKING REVOLUTION: THE INTELLECTUAL HONESTY CHALLENGE

EQUAL HUMAN RIGHTS FOR ALL HUMANS

REALISM VERSUS RELATIVISM

THE THINKING REVOLUTION Unveils the Philosophical Incompatibility Underlying Today's Polarized Politics

WILLIAM BAPTISTE

Human Rights and Freedoms Forever!

THE INTELLECTUAL HONESTY CHALLENGE

HUMAN RIGHTS EDUCATION FOR LASTING FREE DEMOCRACY

FOR EASIER DISTRIBUTION OF ESSENTIAL CONTENT OF THE HUMAN RIGHTS EDUCATION FOR LASTING FREE DEMOCRACY BOOK SERIES, THIS SHORTER BOOK IS DRAWN FROM A KEY CHAPTER IN A LONGER PREVIOUS BOOK IN THE SERIES.

SEND (OR HAND-DELIVER) THE BOOKS TO YOUR ELECTED REPRESENTATIVES AND LEADERS; TO CIVIL SERVANTS, JUDGES, JOURNALISTS, POLICE, MILITARY; TO THOSE IN INFLUENTIAL 'BIG TECH', 'BIG MEDIA,' 'BIG PHARMA' *AND TELL THEM THEY NO LONGER HAVE ANY EXCUSE* TO NOT KNOW AND NOT SUPPORT *THE FOUNDATIONAL PRINCIPLES OF HUMAN RIGHTS AND DEMOCRACY* (AND THE *CORE PRINCIPLES OF LASTING DEMOCRACY*)

Visit William Baptiste's websites at
www.WilliamBaptiste.com
WilliamBaptisteHumanRightsAndFreedomsForever.com

Support Human Rights and Democratic Freedoms for All Humans that Last for Centuries on their Firm Foundations! Volunteer or Donate!
Donations for Democracy can be made at
PayPal.Me/WilliamBaptisteHRAFF
or on the above HRAFF website or email
donate@WilliamBaptisteHumanRightsAndFreedomsForever.com
for more information, more donation options, or to become a VOLUNTEER DEMOCRACY LEADER spreading the essential HUMAN RIGHTS EDUCATION FOR LASTING FREE DEMOCRACY in your area!
Copyright © 2021, 2022 William Baptiste.

REALISM VERSUS RELATIVISM
Unedited Advance Reader Copy, 2nd Printing
Printed in the United States of America
ISBN: 9798488863705

DEDICATION

To all who desire to THINK; So they can learn to do it with intellectual honesty.

Lasting Freedom is the reward of sufficient numbers of honest thinkers.

"Nothing worthy can be built on a neglect of higher meanings and on a relativistic view of concepts and culture as a whole."
— ALEKSANDR SOLZHENITSYN

"The generation now coming out of Western schools is unable to distinguish good from bad. Even those words are unacceptable. This results in impaired thinking ability."
— ALEKSANDR SOLZHENITSYN

". . . We have arrived at an intellectual chaos."
— ALEKSANDR SOLZHENITSYN

CONTENTS

Chapter 1:
Getting to the Very Bottom of the Problem to Solve It
1

Lasting Human Rights and Democratic Freedoms (and Science Itself) Can Only Be Built Upon a Consistent Underlying Philosophical Worldview of Philosophical *Realism*; All Current Threats to Human Rights and Free Democracy (and to Science Itself) Come from Undue Influence of Philosophical *Relativism*.

Chapter 2:
REALISM VERSUS RELATIVISM OVERVIEW **5**

The Top Facts of the History of Philosophy, Most Pertinent to Understanding 21st Century Polarized Western Politics (Rooted in a 17th Century Bifurcation of Philosophy into Two Major Incompatible Streams).

Chapter 3:
Aristotelian Realism is the Fount of the Stream of Western Philosophical Thought Which Begins with the Common Sense by Which All Humans Daily Live Our Lives and Preserve Them from Death; Which has Yielded Science, Logic and Technology **11**

Chapter 4:
Cartesian Skepticism is the Fount of the Stream of Western Philosophical Thought Known As "Modern Philosophy," Which Has Yielded Every Anti-Scientific, Relativistic and Dangerous Philosophy from Solipsism to Marxism Murdering Millions 25

Chapter 5:
The Forgotten History of the Development of Modern Science 37

Chapter 6:
Professor Stephen Hicks, author of *Explaining Postmodernism: Skepticism and Socialism from Rousseau to Foucault*, Explains Why and How Each New Generation of Progressive Socialist Postmodernist Professors has Less Intellectual Capacity and Less Intellectual Honesty with Which to Train the Next Generation after them – *for a Progressive Devolution of Intellectual Quality in Universities* 67

Realism Versus Relativism

Chapter 7:
First Order Questions and Worldview: Why Is There Something Rather Than Nothing? Is Your Worldview Fundamentally Realist (and Scientific) or (Like Marxism's) Radically Skeptical (That Is, Out of Touch with or Denying Reality). Your Politics Follows Suit.
75

Chapter 8:
Science, Medicine, Freedom Threatened by *Relativism not Realism.*
87

Chapter 9:
Some Political Insights Following from The Above Philosophical "Pensées":
Bifurcated, Incompatible Underlying Philosophical Worldviews Lead Ultimately to Today's Polarized Politics Including the Abortion Debate (The Equal Human Rights for All Humans Debate)
99

[Note: This Non-Partisan author, thinker and logician emphasizes that the Abortion Debate (the Equal Human Rights for All Humans Debate) is *not* an issue of political Left versus political Right; but an issue of political *extremism*. The killing of humans by abortion was first legalized in 1920 in *Extremist Left* Marxist (Communist-Socialist) Soviet Russia, before this murderous Extreme Left regime also legalized and carried out the genocide of millions of born humans (legal abortion had already established the government did *not* believe *killing humans is wrong*). The killing of humans by abortion was next legalized in 1934 in *Extremist Right* Fascist Nazi Germany, this murderous Extreme Right regime also legalizing and carrying out the genocide of millions of born humans. Eleanor Roosevelt, a politician of the *real* (not extremist) Left, led the formation of the United Nations' 1948 *Universal Declaration of Human Rights*, of which there is no legitimate nor logical nor intelligent nor intellectually honest interpretation which allows for legal abortion, as abundantly demonstrated within this HUMAN RIGHTS EDUCATION FOR LASTING FREE DEMOCRACY book series.}

Chapter 10:
The Logical Fallacy of *Invalid Appeal to Authority*.
(This is About the Only *Logical Fallacy* in a Logic Textbook Which the Pro-Choice Legal Human-Killing Abortion *Extremist Left* Does *Not* Typically Use to Dishonestly "Defend" Legal Abortion Because They Cannot Find Any Authority Stupid Enough to Claim Abortion is Objectively, Scientifically Good for *Any* of the Humans Involved in It . . .)   **107**

. . . But Pro-Choice Neo-Marxist "Cancel Culture" Leftists Use it to Dishonestly "Defend" Many of Their Other Political Positions; And They Use this Intellectually Dishonest Logical Fallacy to Invalidly and Incorrectly Vilify Anyone Who Disagrees with Them As Somehow "Unscientific" Just for Having a Different Opinion than Themselves, on Topics on Which There is Disagreement Even Among Qualified Experts and Scientists and *Therefore a Non-Expert Citing An Expert Who Happens To Agree with Them Does Not Settle the Issue, Since Qualified Experts Themselves Disagree . . .*

Chapter 11:
Relativism is both Scientifically Stupid and Politically Dangerous because It Does Not Choose Which Differing Subjective Opinion should be Implemented in Public Policy Based on Objective *Facts*; but Rather Only Based on *Power*. (Power via Manipulation; by Threat; or by Violence)   111

Chapter 12:
The GOOD NEWS   117
As the Only-Seemingly-Powerful Totalitarian Relativist Marxist Soviet Union Threatening the World with Nuclear War *Fell Suddenly, Quickly, Bloodlessly* Due to Simple Things Like Solzhenitsyn Merely *Speaking the Truth* Against the Web of Lies that Sustained It; and the *Solidarity Movement* of Soviet-Bloc Citizens who, Despite All Marxist Attempts to Expunge Traditional Western Values, Still Held on to and STOOD UP TOGETHER IN SOLIDARITY FOR the Traditional Western (Judeo-Christian) Values Which Include and Support *The Foundational Principles of Human Rights and Democracy* Identified from Science, Logic, History (and the History of Ideas) in This Book Series;

SO WILL FALL SUDDENLY the Only-Seemingly-Powerful Relativist-Marxist-Influenced "Shroud of the Dark Side, Confusing Everything," Which Solzhenitsyn Warned the West had Infected Western Media and Universities . . . Relativist Threats to Lasting Free Democracy Will Fall Suddenly When Enough People (Embracing *Scientific Realism* Over *Skeptical Relativism*) Simply Speak the Truth Against the Web of Lies and Stand Up *Together* in *Solidarity* to Save Science, Medicine, Freedom in the GLOBAL SOLIDARITY MOVEMENT.

ABOUT THE AUTHOR OF THIS HUMAN RIGHTS EDUCATION FOR LASTING FREE DEMOCRACY   125

YOU Can Help Free Democracy Last Forever!   139
Contact, Donation and Volunteer Support Information

CHAPTER 1
GETTING TO THE VERY BOTTOM OF THE PROBLEM TO SOLVE IT

Lasting Human Rights and Democratic Freedoms (and Science Itself) Can Only Be Built Upon a Consistent Underlying Philosophical Worldview of Philosophical *Realism*; All Current Threats to Human Rights and Free Democracy (and to Science Itself) Come from Undue Influence of Philosophical *Relativism*.

Understanding the History of Ideas (Philosophy) helps one to understand that today's destabilizing political polarization over several issues including the Abortion Debate (The Human Rights for All Humans Debate) is rooted in a bifurcation in Western Thought going back to the 17th Century – a bifurcation fundamentally separating radically *Skeptical, Relativistic* (including Nazi, Marxist, Socialist, *Extremist*) thinkers from *Realist, Scientific* and Logical thinkers.

Meaning everyone should self-reflect and (consciously) identify their (usually unconscious) underlying philosophical worldview (at base predominantly either *Skeptical and Relativistic* or *Realist and Scientific*) so they can make an intelligent decision whether or not they want to keep it in the light of the key facts of Science, Logic, Human Rights History (and the History of Ideas).

CITIZENS AND POLITICIANS HAVING A THOUGHTFUL, CONSCIOUS WORLDVIEW IS PART OF *THE THINKING REVOLUTION* NECESSARY TO ENSURE LASTING FREE DEMOCRACY based on *education*, rather than citizen voters and elected politicians (and unelected bureaucrats/civil servants, judges and journalists and "big tech" billionaires and personnel) with thoughtless *ideology* tearing down Democracy's Realistic, Scientific, and Pro-Life foundations in ignorance.

(Ideologues witlessly destroying Democracy with their uneducated Pro-Choice Legal-Human-Killing Ideology witlessly following 1920 totalitarian Marxist Soviet Legal Abortion precedent;

and/or Neo-Marxist Identity Politics with its "Cancel Culture" censoring ("cancelling") those who disagree with them, *even hard scientists and medical experts* who naturally disagree with the unscientific absurdities of *Relativists Not Realists*;

and/or Radically Skeptical Postmodernist Ideology that denies objective facts and Science, developed by Marxists to protect Marxism from facts).

Note that this book series since *Pro-Life Equals Pro-Democracy* has so overwhelmingly demonstrated that thesis from undisputed facts of Human Rights History, Science and Logic that that book stated from the introduction that the "touchstone democracy test" issue of legal abortion (started in 1920 by *genocidal totalitarian Marxists;* started in 1934 by *genocidal totalitarian Nazis*) is so devoid of factual support that legal abortion is entirely intellectually indefensible in a free democracy and is only supported by the intellectually dishonest (hence *The Intellectual Honesty Challenge* in the book series giving Pro-Choicers the chance to intelligently defend legal abortion in the light of the facts, *if they can* – that is *the challenge.* Literally *every single argument* typically proposed for legal abortion commits at least one intellectually dishonest *logical fallacy,* and dishonestly *avoids the question* of the Human Rights of those humans undisputedly killed in abortions. Meaning that not only do Pro-Choicers not prove their case for legal abortion; they rather prove they do not know how to argue honestly nor logically at all. Abortion is only still legal because the Pro-Choice side has dishonestly ignored the overwhelming facts of Human Rights History, Logic and Science collected in this book series, and refused to ever even have a serious, honest Abortion Debate (Equal Human Rights for All Humans Debate). ***But, while any intelligent person with a decent grip on Reality will easily concede to the overwhelming undisputed facts of Science, Logic and Human Rights History laid out in this book series, there is another, deeper layer to the current problem of Pro-Choice, Neo-Marxist Identity Politics "Cancel Culture" ideologues now ruining many Western governments with 'Creeping Totalitarianism': these ideologues have no grip on Reality because of bad philosophy.*** Underlying the Marxist precedent of legal abortion; and Neo-Marxist Identity Politics; and the "Cancel Culture" which now readily "cancels," censors and censures even qualified experts and scientists who disagree with them, is *the vacuous Postmodernist philosophy developed by Marxists which is so radically philosophically skeptical* that it *denies the existence* of any *objective* facts that can be known and thus absurdly *rejects even Science and Logic*, giving priority to personal, subjective "feelings" and opinions over facts (as an intellectually dishonest way of defending intellectually indefensible Marxism from facts).

CHAPTER 2
REALISM VERSUS
RELATIVISM OVERVIEW

The Top Facts of the History of Philosophy, Most Pertinent to Understanding 21st Century Polarized Western Politics (Rooted in a 17th Century Bifurcation of Philosophy into Two Major Incompatible Streams).

Aristotelian (later Scholastic) Realism Versus Cartesian (later Postmodernist) Skepticism/Relativism: Two Opposed and Incompatible Streams of Western Philosophy Lead Naturally to Today's Bifurcated and Divided Western Politics.

Are you fundamentally a Realist who believes the universe we humans commonly perceive we live in is (objectively) REAL?

Or are you fundamentally a Skeptic who denies or doubts anything outside of your own mind is real (such that you can "create your own reality" and "create your own morality"); such that there is no objective reality but only subjective opinions, such that between any two humans (if other humans than you even exist) there is no objective truth but everything is *relative*?

Aristotelian Realism accords with the Common Sense which keeps humans from dying stupidly, and gave the West Science, Logic, and Technology. The Traditional Western Pro-Life Family Values which include and support *The Foundational Principles of Human Rights and Democracy* were built in the philosophical framework of Aristotelian Realism, and can be scientifically verified as providing the best, healthiest context for new humans to be brought into the world and raised to physically, psychologically and emotionally healthy human maturity in stable, loving families which are the building blocks of politically stable, caring societies.

In contrast, Cartesian Skepticism denies or doubts the certainty of ANYTHING except one's own mind, and gave the West:

Solipsism which denies one can certainly know anything outside one's own mind even exists;

Atheism which (rooted in Skepticism about the universe even existing) denies any Intelligent Orderer of the Universe to account for the intricate order of the universe which may not even exist;

Relativism which denies or radically doubts there are any objective facts (or Science or Logic), accepting only subjective feelings and opinions (because in the skeptical stream of philosophy, only your own mind certainly exists, so why accept any opinions not your own? Without any knowable objective facts, everything is subjective and relative);

Moral Relativism (rooted in Atheist Relativism which doubts or denies objective facts of any kind) which denies any moral absolutes like *Killing Humans is Wrong* or the *Inherent Human Right to Live* or any Human Rights to ground Free Democracy (Note the anti-realist philosophical connection: there were not significant numbers of Atheists until after there were Radical Skeptics denying reality itself exists; there were not significant numbers of Moral Relativists until after there were Relativists denying anything objectively or certainly exists);

Secularism which (adopting Atheist Moral Relativism) claims traditional religious values (including *The Foundational Principles of Human Rights and Democracy* like *Equal Human Preciousness*, which were introduced into the world by Biblical Judeo-Christianity) "have no place in the public sphere;"

Absurdism & Nihilism which deny any objective facts or meaning in the universe;

Existentialism which tries to "assign" meaning to an otherwise uncertain and meaningless universe, with mixed political results for human safety — Existentialist Nietzsche influenced the Nazis; a "successful" Existentialist is merely one who avoids solipsism and suicide by subjectively assigning some kind of meaning to a universe objectively uncertain at best, meaningless and absurd at worst – subjective meaning which can be beneficent (when Existentialists like Kierkegaard assign meaning by embracing Christianity) or murderously totalitarian (Existentialist Marxist Sartre inspired Marxist despot Pol Pot and ¼ of Cambodia died);

Experientialism/Pragmatism which like its root radical Skepticism also prioritizes subjective experience over any scientific notion of objective reality — popularized by Atheist Relativist John Dewey who was extremely influential in (North) American Education, effectively making Atheist Relativist Assumptions ubiquitous in Western "Education," thus "priming" the West for: (Atheist Relativist) Marxism (Communism and Socialism) which unrealistically promises a seductive "classless egalitarian utopia where no-one owns anything and everyone is happy" but which in practice has always resulted in oppressive totalitarian states murdering millions because Atheist Marxism is rooted in Radical Skepticism and Relativism and NOT rooted in reality (unrealistic Marxism has killed more humans than anything else – both born and preborn, the first Marxist State being the first state to legalize abortion, and shortly thereafter the same Marxist State legalized the genocide of this author's ethnic group);

Coming full circle back to the radical philosophical Skepticism which ultimately yielded Atheist, Relativist

Marxism in the first place, Western Marxists in Western universities more recently developed Radically Skeptical Postmodernist Philosophy to save Marxism from the overwhelming facts that Marxism does not work in the Real World (proved by over 94 million killed by Marxist policies in the 20th Century alone), by being so radically skeptical that all facts, science and logic and objectivity are denied (leaving nothing "admissible" to convince today's Neo-Marxist ideologues, who are usually Pro-Choice "Identity Politics" and "Cancel Culture" ideologues, to replace their Marxist-influenced *Ideology* with *Education*);

Nobel Prize-winning Russian author and Historian of Marxism Aleksandr Solzhenitsyn confirmed that Western Education and Media were Marxist-influenced and taking the West towards the same totalitarian ends as in Marxist Soviet Russia, just by a more subtle and insidious route (which can be demonstrated since the 1930s when Western Media hid the Marxist Soviet *Holodomor* genocide of this author's Ukrainian ethnic group in Soviet Marxist Socialist Ukraine – officially known as the Ukrainian Soviet Socialist Republic – Western Media giving the Pulitzer Prize to the dishonest Marxist New York Times journalist who covered up the genocide while discrediting and firing the honest journalists who tried to reveal the genocide while it was happening; and the Western Marxist-influenced Education and Media Solzhenitsyn warned the West about still protects Marxism from facts, which is why everyone knows and rightly abhors the right-wing extremist Nazi atrocities, but hardly anyone knows nor rightly abhors the left-wing extremist Marxist atrocities which killed far more precious humans in more countries than the Nazis ever did – and Marxist ideology still runs rampant in today's Western Pro-Choice Left which follows the original Marxist practice of Legal Abortion, first legalized in Marxist Russia in 1920);

Marxism's latest form, morphing to adapt to new times as Marx himself predicted it would, is Neo-Marxist Identity

REALISM VERSUS RELATIVISM OVERVIEW

Politics, which just like Classic Marxism unrealistically reinterprets all history and toxically bifurcates all past and present societies into adversarial "privileged" and "oppressed" classes, making mutual cooperation for the Common Good based on *Equal Human Preciousness* impossible. Marxist (and Neo-Marxist Identity Politics) thinking by Marx's design exaggerates existing resentments over past (even long past) injustices (like centuries-old slavery) and foments renewed hatred between those labelled "oppressed" and "privileged" specifically in order to create enough political instability to create opportunity for a Marxist takeover of the government. Marx himself considered bloody revolution and violence the necessary first stage of Marxist implementation, and encouraged the violence typically used since in all the genocidal vain attempts to implement the unrealistic "Marxist Egalitarian Utopia" (This typical Marxist pattern is currently demonstrated by the officially Pro-Choice, Identity Politics organization run by self-described Marxists, currently (2020) encouraging riots and burning cars in the U.S.).

The two streams of Western Philosophy which now (after centuries of building up to this) have more or less logically resulted in today's above political polarization which threatens the continuance of Free Democracy and Human Rights are: Aristotelian Realism and Cartesian Skepticism. Today's political differences are literally rooted in a difference between (philosophically speaking) a fundamentally realistic and scientific or else a fundamentally skeptical and relativistic underlying view of the universe or *philosophical worldview.*

CHAPTER 3
ARISTOTELIAN REALISM IS THE FOUNT OF THE STREAM OF WESTERN PHILOSOPHICAL THOUGHT WHICH BEGINS WITH THE COMMON SENSE BY WHICH ALL HUMANS DAILY LIVE OUR LIVES AND PRESERVE THEM FROM DEATH; WHICH HAS YIELDED SCIENCE, LOGIC AND TECHNOLOGY

Aristotelian Realism is the fount of the stream of Western philosophical thought which begins with the Common Sense by which all humans daily live our lives and preserve them from death, by assuming as *First Principles* that the universe/reality we perceive with our senses is indeed *REAL* (with real dangers that can hurt us, like fire and cliffs and buses which might hit us if we step into their path, all of such dangers which we daily avoid through *Common Sense*). Aristotelian Realism which accords with and assumes Common Sense has given us:

- all Western Logic and Science, built on the genius polymath Aristotle's *First Principles of Being/Existence* which precisely describe the orderly nature of the *ordered cosmos* of Reality as humans daily experience it and as Science studies it (such as the Law or Principle of Non-Contradiction, "Something cannot both *be* and *not be* at the same time, and in the same respect." Even in our most fevered dreams, we cannot even *imagine* something that violates this principle of *objective reality*).
- Aristotelian Realism grounds the philosophical school of *Scholasticism* (sometimes called *Thomism* after Saint Thomas Aquinas, Scholasticism's pre-eminent practitioner). *Scholasticism* dominated and characterized the *schools*, that is, the *university system* in Europe from 1100-1700 — up to and including and after the Scientific Revolution which established Modern Science and the Modern Scientific Method within the European universities.
- Aristotelian Realism grounds the Scottish School of Common Sense Realism, which was a Common Sense response to the Radical Skepticism of Scotsman David Hume, who was influenced by Cartesian Skepticism and was the first to take it systematically to some of its more absurd and dangerous conclusions which *divorce human minds from Reality.* In intensely practical terms: humans will die or be seriously injured if they do not consistently concede that there is at least *a strong correspondence* to what we humans commonly *perceive as real* (like sunshine; fire; oceans; other humans; the air we breathe; the bus coming our way) and an *objective external reality* independent of our individual humans minds or

ideas. Scotsman Thomas Reid, the best representative and founder of the School of Common-Sense Realism, wrote:

"... there are certain principles ... which the constitution of our nature leads us to believe, and which we are under a necessity to take for granted in the common concerns of life, without [necessarily] being able to give a reason for them—these are what we call the principles of common sense; and what is manifestly contrary to them, is what we call absurd..."

First Principles in any field of study cannot necessarily be "proven" in a strict sense, nor deduced from other principles, but they can be demonstrated as *necessary* for the field of study to proceed at all. The simple fact is, we humans will die or be seriously harmed (or institutionalized as insane and a danger to self or others) if we do not acknowledge *self-evident aspects of Reality*; if we do not follow Common Sense and treat *commonly experienced reality* as indeed *real.* Common Sense and Science both assume a *high correspondence* between the common human experience of what is real, and the objective reality of Reality. Long before Thomas Reid articulated Common-Sense Realism in response to Modern Philosophy's Cartesian Skepticism as radically articulated by Hume, Aristotle himself noted that those who disagreed with his "First Principles of Being" were still *forced by the ordered nature and structure of reality itself* to act in their *daily* lives *as if he was right.* No matter how fervently anyone denies Aristotelian Realism with their mouths (including today's skeptics and relativists and postmodernists and Marxists and Neo-Marxists — who are all frequently Pro-Choicers), they all live in the same commonly-perceived universe with the rest of us, and they all act *daily* as if Aristotle was right (if they do not, for long enough, they can die very stupidly). Existence itself (Being itself, Reality itself) is structured in such a way (such an ordered, structured way, as *Realism* describes) that you just have to, because Aristotle is *right* in saying things like "something cannot both be and not be at the same time and in the same respect" (and the other of his *First Principles of Being* describing self-evident aspects of Reality which are the starting point for Science). The Principle of Non-Contradiction articulates the ontological/metaphysical reality grounding Science, which has the result in statements that "a statement cannot be both true and false at the same time, and in the same respect" — which grounds Logic, and gives us a way to speak about *Reality* precisely, logically, scientifically, *realistically*.

Daniel J. Sullivan describes the close relationship between Common Sense and Science (and philosophical Realism) more precisely in the following quotation from his 1957 book: *An Introduction to Philosophy: Perennial Principles of the Classical Realist Tradition.* He was very aware of modern non-realist (skeptical and relativist) philosophies which compromised both Science and Common Sense, and therefore he concludes, "Any philosophy, therefore, that strays very far from common sense is suspect. If it goes so far as to contradict the basic certitudes of common sense, then it is guilty of denying reality itself, and on this point common sense can pass judgement on it." In this passage he actually uses the term "philosophy" without specifying he means Realist philosophy (as specified in his subtitle) because he wrote *before* such *unrealistic*, anti-scientific, skeptical and relativistic modern philosophies had yet taken over whole Western universities and governments and cultures/societies. Back when "university-educated" was much more likely to mean one actually had a trained mind with more than just Common Sense, but scientific and

Aristotelian Realism

logical reasoning skills building on Common Sense, as follows:

Common sense refers to the spontaneous activity of the intellect, the way in which it operates of its own native vigor before it has been given any special training. It implies man's native capacity to know the most fundamental aspects of reality, in particular, the existence of things (including my own existence), the first principles of being (the principles of identity, noncontradiction, and excluded middle), and secondary principles (the principles of sufficient reason, causality, etc.)

One of the points that links [Realist] philosophy and common sense is that they both use these principles [articulated clearly by Aristotle, the "Father of Realism," hence starting and grounding all Western Logic, Science, and Technology]. They differ however in the way they use them. Common sense uses them unconsciously, unreflectively, uncritically. They can be obscured or deformed for common sense by faulty education, by cultural prejudices, by deceptive sense imagery. [Realist] Philosophy on the contrary uses these principles critically, consciously, scientifically. It can get at things demonstratively, through their causes. It can therefore defend and communicate its knowledge.

The certainties of common sense, the insights of a reasoning which is implicit rather than explicit, are just as well founded as the certainties of [Realist] philosophy, for the light of common sense is fundamentally the same as that of [Realist] philosophy: the natural light of the intellect. But in common sense this light does not return upon itself by critical reflection, is not perfected by scientific reasoning. [Realist] Philosophy, therefore, as contrasted with common sense is scientific knowledge; knowledge, that is, through causes.

A second point which links [Realist] philosophy and common sense is that they take all reality for their province—common sense blindly, in a kind of instinctive response of the individual to the totality of experience; [Realist] philosophy consciously, in the endeavor to give *every aspect of reality its due. This claim of [Realist] philosophy to know the whole of reality does not mean the [Realist] philosopher makes pretense of knowing everything—the human intellect cannot exhaust the mystery of the smallest being in the universe, let alone everything. It remains true, nevertheless, that all things are the subject matter of [Realist] philosophy, in the sense that the [Realist] philosopher [including scientists, since Natural Science is built on Realism — for centuries in the universities what we call Science was called Natural Philosophy; scientists were called "Natural Philosophers," in the Realist (Aristotelian, Scholastic, Thomist) tradition] takes as his angle of vision or point of view the highest principles, the ultimate causes, of all reality. Along with common sense, then, <u>[Realist] philosophy seeks the comprehensive, all-inclusive view of reality; it is the knowledge of all things.</u> [Realist] Philosophy is thus close to common sense and at the same time different from it. It differs from common sense because it holds its conclusions scientifically, with a clarity and depth inaccessible to common sense. It is close to common sense because it shares the universality of common sense and a common insight into the fundamental structure of reality. We might even say that [Realist] philosophy grows out of common sense, and that common sense taken in its strict meaning is a kind of foreshadowing, a dim silhouette, of [Realist] philosophy proper [and therefore of science proper]. Any philosophy, therefore, that strays very far from common sense is suspect. If it goes so far as to contradict the basic certitudes of common sense, then it is guilty of denying reality itself, and on this point common sense can pass judgement on it.*

Unfortunately, the West would soon after Sullivan's eminently sensible 1957 book, in the 1960s, abandon Traditional Western Values, which were developed in the framework of Realism, as the guide of societal standards and public policy. The West was soon to abandon both Common Sense and (scientific) philosophical Realism (and all objectivity) for radically skeptical (and subjective) philosophical Relativism; the West was soon to abandon the (essentially "Pro-Life," and Judeo-Christian) *Foundational Principles of Human Rights and Democracy* for Atheist Moral Relativism as the new guide for Western society and public policy, in the 1960s Sexual Revolution. The Sexual Revolution which created demand for legal abortion to kill all the unwanted humans naturally produced by immaturely and irresponsibly engaging in Nature's way of generating new precious humans without any intention of doing so. Legal abortion which, the second human-killing abortion was de-criminalized (1969 in the author's country), legally eliminated the *Inherent Human Right to Live* and thus *removed* the solid foundation of all Western rights and freedoms, opening the way for the return of totalitarianism in the West which we are in fact seeing today – for example, this author can be arrested and jailed for peacefully saying "killing humans is wrong because Human Rights are for all humans" anywhere remotely near where humans are being legally killed in violation of their Human Rights; and under several recent laws speaking verifiable science is now a crime when it contradicts the Pro-Choice and other unscientific, relativistic ideologies of Pro-Choice political parties in power. It took this long to start to see the full rotten, anti-scientific and anti-democratic fruit of the Sexual Revolution and the legal abortion it demanded (following the Morally Relativist and genocidal Soviet and Nazi legal abortion precedents) because of centuries of Western good habits of thinking and behaving. Centuries of Western Science built on philosophical Realism and centuries of Western freedom built on *The Foundational Principles of Human Rights and Democracy* were not immediately erased in the West with the Sexual Revolution and legal abortion. But their eventual demise we are now starting to see was made *inevitable* in the present Western Society no longer solidly grounded in Realism nor in *The Foundational Principles of Human Rights and Democracy*.

Dr. Jordan Peterson, my countryman and the world's informal "Professor of Free Speech," in his June 2020 article "The activists are now stalking the hard scientists,"[1] rang the clarion bell to warn us that the so-called "politically correct" (and intellectually *dishonest* or, to use Solzhenitsyn's word, intellectually "*impaired*") Relativist, Neo-Marxist Identity Politics "Cancel Culture" mob, which long ago took over the Social Sciences in most Western universities, are now attacking and punishing the "hard" sciences, the Natural Sciences too – evidently wanting everyone to have brains as untrained, dull and "mushy" as theirs which no longer even benefit from the above-described Common Sense which is the natural gift of humans. For in Sullivan's quote above he noted that the natural human apprehension of those *self-evident aspects of reality* articulated clearly by Aristotle as the First Principles of Being "can be obscured or deformed for common sense by faulty education." Which is clearly the case with the (anti-Realist) Relativist, Marxist-influenced education Solzhenitsyn warned us about in many of today's Western universities, which now churn out supposedly "university-educated" graduates with heads filled with *ideology instead of education*, who are so "dumbed down" by faulty education that many (notably our Pro-Choice legal human-killing politicians) have not only never been trained in logical, intellectually honest thinking, but they have even lost access to humanity's natural gift of Common Sense and its ability to implicitly comprehend self-evident aspects of *reality itself!*

The West, after flirting with Atheist Moral Relativism for a long time (since Atheism's first foray into politics, the

---

[1] https://nationalpost.com/opinion/jordan-peterson-the-activists-are-now-stalking-the-hard-scientists#main-content , accessed July 5, 2020.

bloody French Revolution, and its *Reign of Terror*), in the 1960s finally actually *abandoned* Traditional (democracy-grounding) Western Values, turning the West back towards the primitive and brutal pre-Christian times when human sexuality was completely unrestrained, human-killing abortion was legal, and governments were totalitarian (that is, setting the range of what humans may or may not believe; setting the level of persecution or toleration for humans who did not agree with the government; and holding the power of life and death over the governed: government deciding just what rights humans did or did not have, just when and how just which humans could be killed, without any regard for any *Inherent Human Rights* not given by the government). And you could be arrested and imprisoned for peacefully standing up for the lives of humans the government said it was OK to kill, like I can be so arrested today under current laws passed by philosophically and morally Relativist, Pro-Choice politicians and parties (so uneducated in Human Rights History that they witlessly follow the philosophically *Relativist not Realist* totalitarian Soviet Marxist and Nazi Extremists' precedent of legal human-killing by abortion).

The gradual degradation of Western freedom started accelerating with the 1960s Sexual Revolution which turned sex partners from precious *persons* and life-partners to naturally build a human family with, into mere pleasure *objects* to be selfishly used and then thrown away for the next, *objectified* human pleasure object. The precious human children naturally produced by sex were then also thrown away in human-killing abortion instead of being raised to human maturity lovingly within the *human family* naturally created by the sexual union of the sex partners. Note that cross-culturally and throughout all history (before the recent Sexual Revolution) *marriage* was the universal, cross-cultural social norm for sexual relations, for good reasons rooted in biology itself. Scientifically, biologically speaking, a "successful" sexual encounter is one that produces the next generation of the human species so that the human race continues. Getting pleasure from sexual encounters that do not achieve this vital biological goal is still a legitimate part of marriage which serves biology. Biologically speaking, sex is pleasurable *because* this helps *emotionally bond* the sex partners so they can be loving *mother and father* to any human children naturally produced precisely by their sexual union! Scientifically speaking, sex is pleasurable in order to help form the strong emotional bonds that make a human family (bonds socially confirmed and supported within the wider human community through the universal cross-cultural norm of marriage), *because* the next generation of the human species has by far the *best chance* of growing up safely into a physically, psychologically and emotionally healthy human adulthood within such *stable, loving human families* which are the building blocks of *politically stable, caring human societies.*

Note that Relativist (therefore anti-Realist and anti-scientific) philosopher Karl Marx, in his *Communist Manifesto* and elsewhere, specifically mocked "the traditional family" which is supremely beneficial according to principles of Biological Science. It is thus unsurprising that today's Marxists and Neo-Marxist Identity Politics "Cancel Culture" ideologues who are currently undermining Free Democracy from its very foundations have also abandoned and mocked "the traditional family." "The traditional family" as articulated by traditional Western, Judeo-Christian Pro-Life Family Values which historically helped Western Civilization to grow beyond the brutal, oppressive totalitarianism of the ancient, pre-Christian West, and eventually establish Human Rights and Free Democracy upon Traditional Western Pro-Life Family Values.

ARISTOTELIAN REALISM

It is important to thoughtfully reflect upon human sexuality, in its full emotional and biological power, and to realize that sex which generates human beings is so powerful that any human society's guiding attitude towards sex determines our human destiny as either valuable *persons* to be protected or as *tools* to be used and thrown away. The 2015 Ontario Sexual "Education" curriculum (still in force) teaches young children in Canada's most populous province *that sex is primarily for recreational pleasure* (this "education" was introduced by the most philosophically *Relativist not Realist* and the most totalitarian-oriented government in Canada's history, which passed the first several totalitarian laws which motivated this author's book series HUMAN RIGHTS EDUCATION FOR LASTING FREE DEMOCRACY). *If sex is primarily for recreational pleasure* then other humans are sex objects or *tools* to be used for our pleasure; then the humans produced by sex can be killed by abortion as unwanted tools; and then when human tools no longer serve the State/society the State sanctions their killing by euthanasia (and shames them into asking for it in "assisted suicide") as worn-out tools to be thrown away. But, *if sex is primarily for lifelong-committed loving marriages naturally generating new precious humans in stable loving families (the building blocks of stable loving societies)*, then humans are always valuable *persons* who must never be mere tools for others' sexual pleasure nor mere tools serving a greater State/society, but rather the State is always *obligated* to protect and serve precious human *persons*, which is the necessary foundation for the Human Rights and Democratic Freedoms which only ever developed in Western *Christian* Civilization which lived by this traditional Judeo-Christian sexual ethic and *traditional Family Values.*

So ironically, what the "Sexual Revolution" called the "sexual *repression*" of the traditional, Christian sexual ethic is what brought *real freedom* to unrestrictedly sexual but politically oppressive totalitarian Western Society starting in the 4th Century; and what the "Sexual Revolution" called "sexual *freedom*" is what is bringing back the *real repression* of the ultimately totalitarian or 'Creeping Totalitarian' Pro-Choice philosophy which contradicts the *primary human right to live upon which all Human Rights and Democracy depends.* So-called Christian "sexual repression" *directing* sexuality into *mature* committed loving marriage and family life brought *actual freedom* into Western Civilization, and so-called "sexual freedom" for *immature* sexual pleasure-seeking is bringing back *actual repression* with the compromise of Human Rights and Freedoms for the sake of being able to legally kill the unwanted humans produced by sexual pleasure-seeking *and restricting the democratic freedoms of those medical professionals and other Pro-Life Human Rights advocates who would defend human lives because human lives are always precious.* Once again, scientifically speaking (that is, speaking within the framework of the philosophical *Realism* which grounds Science, *Realism* which more explicitly articulates the self-evident aspects of *reality* which are more implicitly apprehended by the human intellect as Common Sense), sex is pleasurable in order to help form the strong emotional bonds that make a human family (bonds socially confirmed and supported within the wider human community through the universal cross-cultural norm of marriage), *because* the next generation of the human species, biologically speaking, has by far the *best chance* of growing up safely into a physically, psychologically and emotionally healthy human adulthood within *stable, loving human families* which are the building blocks of *politically stable, caring human societies.* It is only philosophical *Relativists not Realists*, whose very grip on *reality* itself (and Science itself; and Common Sense itself) is very weak because of their Relativist (and usually Marxist-influenced) *ideology instead of education*, who are inclined to ignore or doubt the science and sound reason and logic which affirms that Traditional Western Pro-Life Family Values best support human biology for the best physical, psychological and emotional human health, individually and in human society.

In conclusion of this introduction to philosophical Realism and its effects on human society, before below considering philosophical Skepticism and Relativism and their effects on human society:

According to both Common Sense and Aristotelian Realism (and the Scholasticism which assumes both, which dominated the universities until well after Modern Science was created in them), I, the author, indeed exist, as a human being with a human body and mind (in fact, with all the attributes of a human *psyche*, Greek for *soul*, classically understood to include *intellect*, *emotions*, and *will*, all studied in the field of *Psychology*). And all other human beings I perceive around me (and all my readers like YOU) do in fact *exist*. We can only learn to read at all, and understand anything we read, and not die stupidly every day, by assuming, as Aristotelian Realism does, that the universe really exists, and runs according to certain ordered, structured First Principles and Scientific Laws.

The Traditional Western Pro-Life Family Values which include and support *The Foundational Principles of Human Rights and Democracy* (as this book series demonstrates) were built in the philosophical framework of Aristotelian Realism. Moreover, Traditional Western Pro-Life Family Values can be *scientifically verified* as providing the best, healthiest context for new humans to be brought into the world and raised to physically, psychologically and emotionally *healthy human maturity* in *stable, loving families* which are the building blocks of *politically stable, caring societies*. But you can only get such positive political results for countries with millions of humans by treating the world/universe we humans all commonly perceive around us as *Real*.

The natural world/universe around us (our environment) which we constantly respond to and interact with, and which imposes needs for life like air, water, food, *indeed exists.* Therefore, we cannot dispense with eating, drinking or breathing, or else we will die, no matter how much some skeptic Postmodernist and Neo-Marxist professor might have convinced you that "nothing can be known for certain" or that you can "choose your own truth." Such ignorant Postmodernist and/or Neo-Marxist Skeptics and Relativists themselves *all live by Common Sense Realism or else they die*, which is why we can *safely ignore* skeptic Postmodernist and Neo-Marxist professors and "social-justice-warrior" political activists and their claims. In fact, our safety as individuals and as a society depends upon us ignoring and rejecting Radically Skeptical Cartesian, Postmodernist, Atheist, Relativist, Marxist claims and the "ideologically lobotomized" claims of Neo-Marxist Identity Politics with its "Cancel Culture." *Because Cartesian Skepticism is the fount of the stream of Western Philosophical Thought known As "Modern Philosophy," which has yielded every* anti-*scientific, relativistic and dangerous philosophy from Solipsism to Marxism murdering millions.*

CHAPTER 4
CARTESIAN SKEPTICISM IS THE FOUNT OF THE STREAM OF WESTERN PHILOSOPHICAL THOUGHT KNOWN AS "MODERN PHILOSOPHY," WHICH HAS YIELDED EVERY ANTI-SCIENTIFIC, RELATIVISTIC AND DANGEROUS PHILOSOPHY FROM SOLIPSISM TO MARXISM MURDERING MILLIONS

Cartesian Skepticism is the fount of the stream of Western philosophical thought known as "Modern Philosophy." It begins with René Descartes, "The Father of Modern Philosophy," and his famous statement "I think, therefore I am" (French: *"Je pense, donc je suis."* Latin: "*Cogito, ergo sum*"). The statement is first mentioned in a 1637 book; the concept reflected upon in detail in his 1641 book *Meditations.* It was only the second of six meditations presented in the book as taking place over one week, and Descartes himself did not remain so radically skeptical as he is in that meditative intellectual exercise. However, our ideas, good or bad, can take on a life of their own without us, and the practical effect upon history of "I think, *therefore* I am" was unfortunately to *remove all Modern Philosophy after him* from being grounded in *Reality*, by prioritizing *thought* over *being/existence*. This "Cartesian Split," splitting Western Philosophy *away* from Aristotelian Realism's former prioritization of *existence* which gives us Science and technology and accords with the Common Sense which daily keeps us alive, has instead given the West the following long series of problematic philosophical approaches, even the best of which have done great harm:

- *Solipsism* – the philosophical position that (mimicking severe mental illnesses which *divorce the patient from Reality*) denies or seriously doubts that anything or anyone at all exists outside of one's own mind, or can be known to exist for certain.
- *Cartesian Skepticism*, according with Descartes' statement "I think, *therefore* I am" as elaborated in his second of six 1641 *Meditations*, that he could only be absolutely *certain* of the *real* existence of *his own mind* which he knows thinks. Though Descartes himself did not remain so Skeptical (he was too smart for that), he unwittingly opened up Modern Philosophy after him to the most Radical Skepticism of solipsism and every *radical doubting of Reality* position leading up to it, including:
- *Atheism*, which of course denies or doubts the existence of God the (unseen) Creator and Orderer of the Universe (assumed in Aristotelian Realism as the source of the universal, cosmic *order* which Science studies), when Modern Philosophy following Cartesian Skepticism even denies or

doubts the existence of the (seen) physical Universe itself, and denies or doubts the existence of any other minds than one's own! And:
- *Relativism*, which follows from Radical Skepticism and Atheism. Assuming nothing can be known to *objectively* exist for certain, outside of one's own mind, individual *subjects* each *subjectively choose* what they believe exists or does not exist, what is true or not true. Thus, they say unscientific and illogical things like "that's true for *you*, this [contradictory thing] is true for *me,*" violating the Law of Non-Contradiction itself, the first and easiest to prove of *The First Principles of Being* which Science and Logic are built upon. Relativists absurdly deny the easiest to prove Universal Law, ultimately because, as radical Skeptics, they deny any *objective external Reality* (such as recorded facts or observed scientific data) which might furnish tie-breaking *evidence* that one human subject's *opinion* of what is true better accords with *objective external Reality* than another's. Since Relativism denies even the objective physical reality which Science studies with academic rigor, all the more so Atheist Relativism results in:
- *Moral Relativism*, Ethical Relativism, and with it the "impaired thinking ability" Solzhenitsyn points out. Impaired thinking ability which allows solid *education* to be easily replaced by vacuous *ideology*. *Ideology* which has unleashed murderous evil upon the Earth on a scale previously unimaginable. As Solzhenitsyn wrote, "Ideology – that is what gives evildoing its long-sought justification and gives the evildoer the necessary steadfastness and determination. That is *the social theory which helps to make his acts seem good instead of bad in his own and*

others' eyes . . .Thanks to ideology the twentieth century was fated to experience *evildoing calculated on a scale in the millions.*" Many influenced by Relativism try to seem more intelligent and reasonable by claiming they accept scientifically proven realities as *real*, but they consider anything in the moral sphere to be *relative*. Solzhenitsyn would certainly rebuke these in any case (he noted, "those people who have lived in the most terrible conditions, on the frontier between life and death . . . all understand that between good and evil there is an irreconcilable contradiction, that it is not one and the same thing—good or evil—that one cannot build one's life without regard to this distinction. . . "). But moreover, Moral Relativists often have very little understanding of what makes something scientifically proven, and like any Relativist may be prone to simply *claim* things they believe are "scientifically proven." Relativism in general and Moral Relativism in particular are *both* intellectually dishonest and hypocritical. Honestly convinced and consistent Relativists need to be contained in mental health wards for their own safety and that of others; most hypocritically keep alive daily by following Common Sense Realism but still form their political opinions according to incompatible Skeptical Relativism. And no one will scream louder than a Moral Relativist when they think their own rights are being denied (including Moral Relativist Pro-Choice bigots who deny *Equal Human Rights for All Humans* and so are fine with killing preborn humans *in denial of their inherent, equal, inalienable Human Rights*). The huge political danger from Moral Relativists comes from the necessary fact *they can accept no Moral Absolutes* like *killing humans is wrong* nor any *Inherent Human Rights* which governments are obligated to protect; nor can they accept any authority higher than the government to which the government is *accountable* for how it treats the humans it governs. Which is why all the representatives of Atheist, Relativist, Marxist countries on the United Nations' original Human Rights Commission refused to even vote on the UN's magnificent 1948 *Universal Declaration of Human Rights* (and why all Marxist States have committed millions of murders). Atheism, rooted in the Radical Skepticism made possible by Descartes and Modern Philosophy, has given the West:

- *Secularism*, which proceeds from Atheist Relativism, especially Moral Relativism, meaning no moral absolutes *like killing humans is wrong* can be consistently applied or else secularists complain of "religious values in the public sphere" (religious values like *Equal Human Rights for All Humans* and all of *The Foundational Principles of Human Rights and Democracy*, which are specifically Biblical and Judeo-Christian in origin – as is the key insight of the Aristotelian philosophical Realism which grounds all Science, that the universe is an *ordered cosmos* and *not* a *random, undirected chaos*, which is *why* Nature is susceptible to scientific studies that reveal the underlying *orderliness* of the universe. And which is *why* the Modern Pure Sciences and the Modern Scientific Method only developed in Christian Europe which built itself deliberately on Biblical insights).
- Such Atheist Relativism, rooted in the Radical Skepticism made possible (if unwittingly) by

Descartes, and by how Modern Philosophy unfortunately developed after him, has, unfortunately, above all given the West below-described *Marxism* (Communism/ Socialism), Atheism's by far most sophisticated and popular political theory for organizing human societies – utterly rooted in *Skeptical Relativism* and utterly incompatible with *Scientific Realism*, which is why Marxism *never works in the Real World*, but consistently has distinctly the *opposite* of its claimed intended effects of "making the world a better, more equal, place" where "no-one owns anything and everyone is happy" under highly centralized State control of resources (in theory, equitably distributed). But Marxist, Socialist States always consistently devolve into what Solzhenitsyn described as merely "the equality of destitute slaves" (the world's first Marxist State, the Union of Soviet Socialist Republics/USSR organized around Soviet Russia, actually first *legalized human-killing* by abortion, *and then by genocide*!). One of Marxism's many flaws is that because it requires tight State control of resources and so on it cannot tolerate normal free-thinking variety of opinions, nor free speech that criticizes just how the State goes about its tasks and so countless individuals always get imprisoned or executed "for the good of the State." Solzhenitsyn's *The Gulag Archipelago* describes how the ravenous gulag prison system in the world's first Socialist Marxist Relativist State had to be set up almost immediately. But Marxist-influenced ideologues, because they are Relativists who *reject objective facts* in favor of *subjective feelings and opinions*, are rarely *swayed* by these *facts* to abandon Marxism.

Instead, they just brainlessly spread Marxism in newer forms, yielding Marxism's immense current popularity in the West (especially in its newer form of the Neo-Marxist Identity Politics which Solzhenitsyn commented on in a 1983 speech, wherein he noted *"Atheist teachers in the West are bringing up a younger generation in a spirit of hatred of their own society . . ."* Solzhenitsyn, the world's foremost expert on Soviet Marxism, living 18 years in the U.S., confirmed that U.S., Western mainstream media and education were Marxist-influenced and were taking the West towards the same ultimately totalitarian ends as Marxism took his beloved Russia – just by a different, more subtle and insidious route. This current, ultimately anti-democratic Atheist Relativist Marxist influence in the West was greatly facilitated by the previous Western popularity of:

(Atheist, Relativist) *Pragmatism/ Experientialism,* which is rooted in Atheist Relativism and like it emphasizes *subjective experience* as having priority over any Realist and Scientific notions of *objective Reality* (which approach, of course, ultimately goes back to Descartes' unwitting introduction of *radical skepticism* into Western Philosophy, which came precisely from Descartes (in his second *Meditation* of six) giving his own *subjective experience* and his personal, subjective ability to *think* about it priority over any notion of *objective existence* independent of his own mind — as in his famous but erroneous statement, "I think, *therefore* I am," which in practical effect *unhinged from Reality* "Modern Philosophy" after Descartes, by doubting any possible *certainty* outside one's own mind and thought. Hence, to a *pragmatist*, only what is (subjectively) *experienced* is "real," and (pragmatically) "truth" is just "whatever works." Because Science works so consistently well, Pragmatism inconsistently tries to incorporate science, using it just "because it works," while *inconsistently denying* Science's actual foundations in philosophical (Aristotelian, Scholastic, Thomist) *Realism* - absurdly denying *why* Science works, which is because Science's underlying worldview and *First Principles* accord with the *objective Reality of the universe* which Science studies as *real, objective* and existing *independently* of our subjective minds and experience. What makes Pragmatism/Experientialism (sadly) important to the current threats to Free Democracy (and to Scientific thinking, where in the author's country people can now be arrested or hauled in front of a tribunal for speaking verifiable scientific facts which do not support the new-fangled anti-scientific ideologies of Pro-Choice Left governments) is that the primary promoter of this Pragmatist, Relativist philosophical worldview was John Dewey (1859-1952).

Dewey was hugely influential in American education, and well beyond America's borders. **Devoutly Atheist (and Relativist), he was one of the signers of the original 1933 Atheist *Humanist Manifesto,* which at the time honestly described Atheist *Secular Humanism* as an *Atheistic religion* intending to replace traditional "theistic" religions (such devout Atheists later realized that they could get a lot more influence in Western society than their tiny numbers deserved, a kind of "Atheist Apartheid," by *pretending* that Atheism was *not* ultimately just another underlying *religious worldview* accepted on *faith not proof* (in the non-existence of any Orderer God who gave the universe its *intricate order* which Science studies only because of its *First Principles* which from the beginning of Science *assumed* such an Orderer); and by *pretending* that traditional theistic religions *"had no place in the public sphere"* — even though nothing could be more asinine, since, as this book series demonstrates, Traditional Western (Judeo-Christian) Pro-**

CARTESIAN SKEPTICISM

Life Family Values include and support *The Foundational Principles of Human Rights and Democracy* without which (see Chapter 2) the West *could never have developed* and is *predictably losing* its traditional Human Rights and freedoms – and this author can now be arrested in Canada for peacefully saying "killing humans is wrong because Human Rights are for all humans" under current provincial laws passed in mere *weeks* (in 2017) or *days* (in 2020) by *officially Pro-Choice*, effectively *Neo-Marxist Extremist Left* philosophically *Relativist instead of Realist* political parties in power).

Atheist Relativist Dewey's vast educational influence in the West thus popularized the *myth of opposition* between (Judeo-Christian) Faith and (Scientific) Reason. A vacuous myth *which could only be believed by someone utterly uneducated in the actual, utterly Judeo-Christian and Theistic history of Science* from ancient (Theistic) Aristotle to the (all devoutly Christian) founders of Modern Science and the Modern Scientific Method in the Scientific Revolution which occurred only in the Christian universities of Christian Europe (which had themselves organically grown out of the Medieval Christian "Cathedral Schools" which had started with intense scholarly study of the Bible and then branched out into all other fields of knowledge – **all motivated by the ancient Jewish and Christian** *scholarly emphasis* **on the** *search for objective Truth in all its forms* (which had made Aristotle's famous pupil Alexander the Great put the scholarly Jews in charge of the great ancient Library of Alexandria in Egypt, which Alexander had named after himself). But such *facts* do not matter at all to at bottom Skeptic Atheist, philosophical Relativists who *deny any objective facts* in favor of mere *subjective feelings and opinions* – including experientialists/pragmatists like preeminent American "educator" John Dewey.

Thus, entirely *ignorant* of Science's historical and logical foundations and without any real motivation to trade their current *ideology* for actual *education,* Atheist Relativists (like John Dewey was) are simply *ignorant* of the *facts* that Aristotle's *First Principles of Being/Existence* which underlie all Western Science, Logic, and Technology merely expanded the prior essentially *Biblical* insight Aristotle's ancient Socratic School had been previously exposed to, that the Universe is an "*ordered cosmos"* with an intelligent Orderer (and NOT an ultimately "*random, undirected chaos").* Thus, entirely *ignorant* of Science's historical and logical foundations and without any real motivation to trade their current *ideology* for actual *education,* Atheist Relativists (like America's top "educator" John Dewey was) are simply *ignorant* of the *facts* of the *formation of Modern Science and the Modern Scientific Method* by the devoutly Judeo-Christian *theists* of the 16th and 17th Century Scientific Revolution (like Copernicus, Kepler, Galileo, Sir Francis Bacon and Sir Isaac Newton) working from *key insights* the West originally learned *from the Bible (Jewish Bible/Christian Old Testament),* expanded by ancient (Greek Socratic School) *Theist* Aristotle into *The First Principles of Being/Existence* such as the Law of Non-Contradiction, which *make all Western Science, Logic, and Technology possible.*

Of course, John Dewey and today's similarly Atheistic, Relativistic "thinkers" (I must use the term only *loosely* because of their manifest *intellectual dishonesty*) are apparently completely *ignorant* of the fact Greek Aristotle was preserved from the so-called "Dark Ages" following the Western, Latin-speaking Roman Empire's 476 AD destruction at the hands of overwhelming barbarian tribes, in the Eastern, Greek-speaking Roman (Byzantine) *Christian* Empire which lasted for another 1000 years, until its 1453 conquest by the Muslim Turkish Ottoman Empire.

Cartesian Skepticism

The Christian Church in Ukraine (this author's faith tradition) was originally evangelized by ancient Greek-speaking Christianity in 988 AD, when all of Ukraine whole-heartedly underwent mass Christian baptisms in rivers – so completely and honestly embracing Christianity that it is impossible to speak of the history of Ukraine since without referencing the Christian Church. Which is why the Relativist Atheist Marxists/ Communists/ Socialists who militarily conquered the briefly independent Ukraine went to such lengths as committing the 1932-33 *Holodomor* ("Murder by Starvation") Genocide against this author's fellow Ukrainian, Eastern Rite Christians (mostly rural farmers. This author's Ukrainian Greek Catholic Church later became the largest underground Church of the 20th Century: it officially *did not exist* under Soviet Communism but emerged 5 million strong when the Socialist Soviet Union dissolved)[2]. The *Holodomor* was after they had killed the Russian Tsar who had ruled both Russia and Ukraine for centuries, and after they in the bloody 1917 "Great October Socialist Revolution" (months after Solzhenitsyn's conception) had firmly established philosophically *Relativist not Realist*, Atheist Marxist Communist Socialists into sole ruling political power for the first time. The Relativist Atheist Marxist Soviets had to murder an estimated 7-10 million of my Ukrainian ethnic group in the *Holodomor* Genocide in order to break the Christian spirit of Ukraine to resist Relativist Atheist Socialists who (just like Neo-Marxist Identity Politics "Cancel Culture" Socialists today) were attempting to rewrite history and culture in

---

[2] There were (and are), of course, many more than five million underground Christians in Marxist, Communist, Socialist China – but they belong to hundreds or thousands of the tens of thousands of splintered denominations or sects of Western Rite Christianity since Western Rite Christianity's Protestant Reformation, and thus there are not so many as five million Chinese Christians from any one Christian denomination/sect, which is why this author can confidently refer to Eastern Rite Christianity's Ukrainian Greek Catholic Church as the largest underground Church of the 20th Century, 5 million coming up from the underground when Soviet Marxism in Ukraine ended – plus more than that many in the worldwide Ukrainian diaspora, which includes more Ukrainians in this author's country of Canada than any other country outside Ukraine.

Marxist terms of "oppressed class rejecting and overthrowing previous 'privileged/oppressor' class in order to establish Marx's egalitarian utopian vision"). The Atheist Soviet (and later Atheist Chinese, Vietnamese, Cambodian, Korean, etc.) *philosophically Skeptical and Relativistic Marxists*, who explicitly deny the (Aristotelian and Scholastic) philosophical *Realism* which grounds all Scientific enquiry, throughout the 20th Century could not accept the *facts* and tremendous evidence that despite their best attempts to realize the *unrealistic* Marxist utopian vision, Marxism just does not work in the *Real World* – because they were *Relativists not Realists,* who believe in *subjective opinion* over *objective facts* (which Relativists deny, instead accepting contradictory absurdities like "that's true for you; this contradictory thing is true for me"). And because Relativists who think even facts are "relative" are usually Moral Relativists as well, they had no moral problem murdering many millions of Ukrainian humans in order to help set up the world's first State run by Relativist Atheist Marxist Socialist "thinkers," the Union of Soviet Socialist Republics (USSR). Other Relativist Atheist Marxists later had no problem killing one quarter of Cambodia's population, and committing countless atrocities in Vietnam, North Korea (etc.) while still trying to implement unrealistic Marxism in the Real World. And the Marxist-influenced today still claim everyone else who has tried to establish a Marxist utopia before just somehow did it wrong when *every single attempt descended into murderous totalitarian oppression*, but they will (somehow) succeed! Marxist (and today's Pro-Choice Neo-Marxist Identity Politics "Cancel Culture") ideologues just keep trying to hammer (and sickle) the "Red Square peg" of Marxism into the "round hole" of *reality*, no matter how many precious humans (born and preborn) are killed in the attempts. It is difficult to convince them to stop trying (and stop hurting humans) because their brains barely function due to the "ideological lobotomy" or "impaired thinking ability" due to Relativism of which Solzhenitsyn spoke. Because as philosophical *Relativists not Realists*, they just do not have any solid grip on *Reality*.

CHAPTER 5
THE FORGOTTEN HISTORY OF THE DEVELOPMENT OF MODERN SCIENCE

But, thankfully for Western Science and Technology (and freedom!), Eastern, Greek Rite Christians (like this author!) preserved ancient Greek Aristotle, "the Father of Realism," and "the Father of Science," so that after the "Dark Ages" following the barbarian conquest of the Western Roman Empire, Aristotle could be re-introduced into the West in the new (medieval) Western university system, which was the fertile intellectual ground where the introduction of the "Father of Realism" Aristotle *made Science as we know it take off by leaps and bounds.*

Ignorant Atheists simply know almost nothing of the origins and logical development and establishment of Science (by religious believers and absolutely no Atheists) from ancient through to modern times. This author respects intellectually honest Atheists and loves to have intelligent dialogue with them (I have even gained personal friends this way, despite our differing positions). Intellectually honest scholars who are Atheists (like historian Tom Holland) have been honestly writing about the importance of traditional Christianity to the development of Human Rights and freedoms (which cannot possibly be denied by any honest intellect, as abundantly demonstrated in this book series).

However, as shown above, Atheism itself is rooted in (intellectually dishonest and ultimately anti-scientific) radical Skepticism and Relativism. So, the typical Atheist is not intellectually honest. Whether in officially Atheist countries, which are always oppressive and murderously totalitarian; or whether here in the traditionally "Free West," which they foolishly often wish were Atheist countries – typical Atheists learned from their Atheist mentors to "fart with their brains" their insubstantial yet often viciously condescending "Atheistic flatulence" that demeans religious believers as somehow "backwards" and "unscientific" and somehow having "no place in the public sphere" (despite Christianity specifically introducing the West to *The Foundational Principles of Human Rights and Democracy*). Typical Atheists learned this intellectually dishonest, offensive and ultimately democracy-destroying attitude from their Atheist mentors *instead* of learning how to think and reason clearly, consistently, logically and with intellectual honesty, from *First Principles* through to sound conclusions – something their typical Atheist mentors had no idea how to do. So, typical wind-bag Atheists idiotically claim religious believers are somehow "unscientific" only because typical Atheists *know almost nothing* of the history of Science discussed in this author's book *DEMOCRACY 101* (citing an eminent scientist who actually knows the history of his field), as in this brief excerpt from *DEMOCRACY 101:*

... the whole modern university system historically grew out of Christian Europe's medieval cathedral schools, first dedicated to scholarly Bible study which then branched out into all the other fields of knowledge and scholarship. Theology – The Study of God and All Things in Relation to God – was historically "the Queen of the Sciences" and Christian "religious colleges" are still at the core of all the oldest and most established universities today. The University of Paris, also known as the Sorbonne, grew out of the Notre Dame de

Paris Cathedral School. The central College of Sorbonne was one of its colleges of Theology. Doctoral degrees were first introduced here. Note that the Latin word scientia means "knowledge" – at base a science is simply a field of knowledge, which is why we speak of "social sciences" and "human sciences" which include psychology. Theology was known as "the Queen of the Sciences" because it included all other fields, being the formal study of God and all things in relation to God – a broad field without the narrow focus of some fields but yielding a wide berth of knowledge in many fields.

Today, when we say "Science" in English and other languages, we usually mean natural science or the Science of Nature, those sciences or fields of knowledge like Physics, Chemistry, and Biology which study some aspect of Nature. The "Pure" (Natural) Sciences study and observe nature purely for its own sake; for whatever can be discovered about nature; the "Applied" (Natural) Sciences apply what has been discovered about nature to useful purpose including the "Industrial" Science of making things which we call technology. For centuries in universities this that we now call Science was called "Natural Philosophy," and the highest level or doctoral degree (doctor is Latin for teacher) in the Natural Sciences (as in other fields) is still called a "Doctor of Philosophy" degree (Ph.D. for short). Stephen M. Barr (Ph.D. – his is from Princeton University where he was awarded a fellowship "for distinguished research") is a practicing scientist who does research in theoretical particle physics and cosmology, and is Professor of Physics at the University of Delaware; and he is also someone who has actually bothered to learn the history of the Science he makes such distinguished use of and so does not make the grossly ignorant and uneducated statements Atheist scientists frequently do. In his short 2011 book Science and Religion: The Myth of Conflict ... after noting the two now-discredited late-19th Century (one-century old) books which have been identified as being most responsible for the current popularity and the current form of the Enlightenment-era (two-century old)

Cartesian Skepticism

Myth of the Conflict Between Science and Religion, Professor Barr notes the historical reality:

"The medieval [Christian] universities were the first institutions in human history where science was studied and taught on a continuous basis from generation to generation by a stable community of scholars. Before this, it had always depended on the whims of wealthy and powerful individuals. As the noted historian of Science Prof. Edward Grant put it, the medieval universities "institutionalized" science. Moreover, they produced hundreds of thousands of graduates, who were introduced to scientific questions and from whose ranks scientific talent could emerge. The scientific community and the scientific public created by the medieval universities were the soil in which the seeds of the Scientific Revolution germinated. Most of the great figures of the Scientific Revolution were educated in universities that had been founded in the Middle Ages."

That is to say, most of those most responsible for the modern Scientific Method were trained in Science at universities that grew out of the Christian cathedral schools and which for centuries had been taught by Christian priests and monks who had studied Science as a prerequisite for studying Theology. As the following Articles [in the author's book DEMOCRACY 101] will elaborate, those most responsible for modern Science (and the modern Scientific Method) were devout Christians (both Catholic and Protestant) – and absolutely no Atheists! And far from Christianity being a detriment to scientific enquiry, the Judeo-Christian Biblical Revelation of a Creator God who ordered the Natural Universe actually spurred the European scientific quest to find patterns of order in nature, which is why the Pure Sciences and the modern Scientific Method developed only in Christian Europe and NOT the Far East – the Far Eastern religious traditions had no rational, intelligent orderer God to set up the universe with rationally discernible Laws, so no attempt was made to look for such Laws, even though otherwise they were capable of the detailed observations of nature which Science requires

and occasionally made discoveries about nature based on these. Yet developed no systematic Pure Sciences as developed only in Christian Europe! The Far East only had the Applied Sciences like Engineering, wherein human ingenuity applied to very practical problems used whatever was known to build gradually better bridges, buildings, and weapons. Western technology eventually outdid all others because the vast intricate detail about the natural universe discovered by the Western Pure Sciences "super-charged" what the Applied Sciences – including the Industrial Science of Technology – had to work with. And Christian scientists are operating from the same basic worldview of an ordered cosmos (not random chaos) with an intelligent orderer when they are in labs doing science and when they are worshipping in Church and practicing their beliefs, which cannot be said of religious Atheist scientists and those of other (non-Abrahamic) religions, whose religious faith operates from a different basic worldview than that which they use in a science lab – Atheists having merely borrowed the Scientific Method from the Christians who developed it, and those in countries without an Abrahamic Faith tradition having merely adopted Western Science (as it was fully-formed by the Christian West) without understanding its underlying Judeo-Christian First Principles.
– *William Baptiste, DEMOCRACY 101, citing Dr. Stephen M. Barr*

Atheist Relativists and Pragmatists like Dewey, with their *ideology instead of education*, just do not know nor "get" any of the above. Thus, Pragmatism (Experientialism) and John Dewey's (unfortunately) extremely influential use of it in American education is largely responsible for the "dumbing down" of (North) American education, by replacing the underlying worldview of traditional Scientific Realism from which we get Science, Logic (and ultimately technology) with an unstable and illogical underlying worldview of Atheist Relativism — Pragmatism/Experientialism actually bringing to the forefront of

CARTESIAN SKEPTICISM

"education" the "subjective experience over objective reality" by which Descartes foolishly (accidentally) unhinged Western thought from Scientific Realism in the first place. *After the devout Christians of the Scientific Revolution* like like Copernicus, Kepler, Galileo, Sir Francis Bacon and Sir Isaac Newton had done most of their work in founding Modern Science. Of these, only Isaac Newton had not yet already finished his contribution to Modern Science and the Modern Scientific Method when Descartes first published his *Meditations*, the second of six *meditations* which had the unfortunate effect of popularizing the erroneous and anti-Realist, anti-Scientific conclusion, "I think, *therefore* I am." Of course, Newton and all Western Science since *ignored* the Radical perceptual Skepticism unwittingly unleashed into "Modern Philosophy" by Descartes (who did not remain in radical Skepticism himself – he was indeed too smart for that).

This is why absolutely no Atheists were involved at any stage of the development of Science, nor of the Modern Scientific Method: precisely because Atheism is historically and logically rooted in Radical Skepticism and Relativism; precisely because Atheists effectively deny the universe is an ordered cosmos (which implies an intelligent Orderer), and instead assert the opposite, that the universe is ultimately entirely random and undirected by any God — leaving no reason to look for *patterns of order* in Nature as did all the theists (mostly Christians) who *actually developed Science* from ancient to modern times. Theists including Aristotle, the "Father of Realism" and the "Father of Science." The brilliant ancient Greeks of his Socratic School rejected the traditional pagan Pantheon of "gods" on Mount Olympus (Zeus, Apollo, Aphrodite etc.) as *silly superstition*, but *worshipped* the *Absolute Being* (Who necessarily exists; Who *is* existence itself) upon whom all *contingent beings* depend (*contingent*; unnecessary and changeable beings who did not always exist and may go in or out of existence, including planets and humans). Science is specifically the study of (material) *contingent* existence brought into being by and *ordered* intelligently by the Absolute Being, who necessarily exists and cannot not exist.

So, Atheist Relativist "Experientialist/Pragmatist" John Dewey, possibly the most influential "educator" in American history steeped (North) American education in the same Atheistic Relativism (itself steeped in Radical Skepticism) in which oppressive totalitarian States (especially Marxist Socialist States) are. Ultimately anti-scientific Philosophy that makes a mockery and a joke out of today's Western educational system — and which is driving us towards the totalitarian future Aleksandr Solzhenitsyn predicted precisely because of such Atheistic Relativism which destroyed his country too. Atheistic Relativism which is today still producing mush-for-brains anti-scientific Relativists with what Solzhenitsyn called "impaired thinking ability." Such that even the supposedly "university educated" can no longer understand basic science like the fact *preborn humans are humans* and therefore *abortion kills humans* (with massive intellectual dishonesty, Pro-Choice politicians will avoid admitting this simple science if they can get away with it); nor can they even understand a basic, perfectly sound and scientific logical syllogism like *All Humans have Human Rights. Preborn humans are humans. Therefore, preborn humans have Human Rights.* Nor do they even understand basic Biological Science like that in mammalian and other species, males are males, females are females, with real biological differences that are important to the survival of the species. *Objective scientific facts* (like *maleness* and *femaleness* are encoded in the DNA in *every cell* of a mammal's body) mean nothing to philosophical Relativists to whom everything is *subjective opinion* and therefore *personal choice*, however. But this Relativistic lack of intelligent, scientific understanding does not just make

CARTESIAN SKEPTICISM

Relativists silly people, unfortunately. No, they are also ultimately *dangerous* silly people, because this Relativism is the same underlying bad philosophy that underlies Atheist totalitarian Marxist Communist Socialist ideologues, and thus, like them today's Pro-Choice anti-scientific Relativist politicians have no problem passing laws and policies against Free Speech of verifiable science, wherever science does not support totalitarian ideologies. Totalitarian ideologies including totalitarian "Pro-Choice" legal human-killing abortion ideology, which follows the 1920 totalitarian extremist Left-wing Soviet Marxist and 1934 totalitarian extremist Right-wing Nazi Fascist precedents of legal human-killing abortion. "Pro-Choice" Relativists (and pragmatists) easily kill humans following evil Soviet and Nazi precedents because nothing at all is *evil* when everything is *relative*, and because everything, even human-killing, comes down to personal "choice" for a subjectivist (experientialist/pragmatist) Relativist (including Moral Relativist) and philosophical *Skeptic* who at bottom is not even *certain* anything outside of his or her own mind even exists, after all. But Solzhenitsyn reminds us:

"... those people who have lived in the most terrible conditions, on the frontier between life and death, be it people from the West or from the East, all understand that between good and evil there is an irreconcilable contradiction, that it is not one and the same thing— good or evil—that one cannot build one's life without regard to this distinction. I am surprised that pragmatic philosophy consistently scorns moral considerations; and nowadays in the Western press we read a candid declaration of the principle that moral considerations have nothing to do with politics. I would remind you that in 1939 England thought differently. If moral considerations were not applicable to politics, then it would be incomprehensible why England went to war with Hitler's Germany. Pragmatically, you could have gotten out of the situation, but England chose the moral course,

and experienced and demonstrated to the world perhaps the most brilliant and heroic period in its history."
— *Aleksandr Solzhenitsyn*

Hence, *before* Moral Relativism and everything that comes with pragmatist/ experientialist skepticism/ relativism and *subjectivism over objectivity* (planted firmly in North American education by pragmatist John Dewey) grew up and took hold of the West by the time of the 1960s Sexual Revolution, Western nations like England *still had the moral compass and fortitude of character* to militarily oppose Adolf Hitler's bigoted *Extremist* Right-wing Nazi Fascist regime which rejected Traditional Western Values including the *equal human preciousness* that undergirds free democracies. Which is why England declared war on Nazi Germany and led the Allied nations in the successful fight for freedom built on Traditional Western Values. But *after* Moral Relativism and everything that comes with the pragmatism now in Western schools took its grip on Western society and culture, the West *freely followed Nazi Extremist precedents* and legalized human-killing abortion (and later legalized human-killing euthanasia). *Before* Moral Relativism rooted in philosophical Skepticism became a feature of Western culture in the Sexual Revolution which formally abandoned democracy-grounding Traditional Western Values, the Free West still had enough gumption to declare war on Nazi Germany to protect humanity from Nazi legal human-killing evil. Including legal abortion and euthanasia for which Nazi doctors were condemned at the Nuremberg War Crimes Trials, because these were recognized as further Extremist Nazi *crimes against humanity* which criminally violated the Human Responsibility to recognize and protect Human Rights in all other humans. But *after* Moral Relativism became a feature of Western culture, the West started *freely, willfully* taking on these evil human-killing practices which the evil Nazis would have *forced* upon the Free West if the Nazi Extremists had won World War II! And the ultimate result of such Moral Relativism is, predictably, the ultimate loss of our Western freedoms to legal human-killing political extremism.

Thus, in 2015, in my country's most populous province doctors had their Freedom of Conscience and Religion – and their freedom to practice the ancient *non-killing* (Hippocratic) Medical Profession – taken away by policies forcing them against their conscience to facilitate human-killing abortion and newly-legalized human-killing euthanasia. At the end of a public monthly meeting organized by local doctors in January 2015, when there was news of this impending policy, the main doctor asked me to address the crowd about the problem after the regular itinerary was finished. I said in my address "this is the line in the sand. If they get away with this policy, religious freedom is on the way out. The attacks will not stop there." Someone from the crowd humorously suggested later that, being winter in Canada, it was actually "the line in the snow." Much later the provincial Superior Court actually admitted that policies and legislation since 2015 requiring Pro-Life (Traditional Hippocratic) doctors to facilitate human-killing abortion and euthanasia against their conscience do in fact violate doctors' Freedom of Religion which is supposed to be guaranteed in the Canadian Charter of Rights and Freedoms. Yet the Court still judged that this suppression of doctors' democratic freedoms of Conscience and Religion was somehow *acceptable* in the case of making doctors provide "healthcare." What Solzhenitsyn called the "impaired thinking ability" of *Relativism* even in otherwise intelligent educated officials (who still lack the HUMAN RIGHTS EDUCATION FOR LASTING FREE DEMOCRACY identified from History, Science, Logic and Philosophy in this book series) means stupid judgements from courts. In what *objective reality* could killing humans be reasonably called "healthcare"? "Healthcare," for those too ideologically lobotomized to know, is supposed to improve the overall health of humans, not to end their health and their lives. For 2500 years the ancient Hippocratic Medical Tradition to "do no harm" meant *doctors do not kill* – and whenever a pregnant woman came into a doctor's office, the doctor as a rule understood he or she had *two patients*. The oldest forms of the Hippocratic Oath specifically prohibited human-killing abortion and euthanasia. But to a Relativist with little grasp on any objective reality, it is easy to merely *label* what is in precise scientifically verifiable fact *human-killing abortion* which typically dismembers, decapitates and disembowels unique humans as "healthcare." How can killing a unique individual human life with absolutely unique human DNA reasonably be called "healthcare" at all, never mind using this dishonestly misdefined "healthcare" as an excuse to trample doctors' normal (and supposedly constitutionally guaranteed) democratic freedoms of conscience and religion? But deep-down philosophical *Relativists not Realists* have no good sense of history, science, or logic, so Relativist-influenced judges all over the world find it really easy to mangle and ignore the democratic constitutions of their particular country by simply (and with intellectual dishonesty) relabelling important terms as something they are not, according to their *ideology not education*; or misinterpreting their nation's (and the United Nations') founding democratic documents without any educated nor intelligent appreciation of the original historical context in which these documents were written – documents which, properly and contextually interpreted, were intended to keep the future of these democracies democratic! But today, fundamentally Relativist and/or Marxist-Socialist-influenced ideologues in positions of authority interpret founding democratic documents however they like, to the detriment of their democracies; and to the detriment of the United Nations; noticeable above all in the ways that today's nations and United Nations shamelessly promote the legal human-killing by abortion first legalized by the oppressive totalitarian Soviets and Nazis *who did not believe killing humans is wrong*; in utter denial of any *inherent, equal, inalienable Human Rights* which ground lasting free democracies.

All the way back in 2015 when doctors' freedom of conscience and religion was taken away (this violation later upheld by a Relativist – therefore incompetent – Superior Court), I then predicted my current reality of the last several months (at time of writing), where I and over 5 million other people have (just like in Marxist totalitarian States!) been banned by the government from holding or attending any public worship service (using the Coronavirus Pandemic as an excuse), *while we are allowed to attend secular activities with hundreds of other people at a time*, in crowded malls, restaurants and fun centers and museums and so on. Back in 2015 I said that the governments passing the kinds of totalitarian laws and policies against Freedom of Religion I first saw in 2015 would take advantage of any later instability, like a war *or a pandemic*, to oppress religious freedom even more. And just recently (at time of writing) I was in a provincial Supreme Court observing the proceedings of a constitutional challenge to the bigoted double standard of "Coronavirus Measures" restricting sacred activities much more harshly than secular activities, wherein the Supreme Court's final judgement, like the boneheaded and bigoted judgement against doctors' rights above, again admitted that the government policy clearly did infringe on constitutionally guaranteed freedoms of religion, speech, assembly and association, *but somehow nevertheless were justified.* When such a bigoted double-standard for secular versus sacred activities could never be reasonably justified by the Coronavirus Pandemic, because a virus follows biological not spiritual laws and will not spread any more nor any less based on whether the purpose of a gathering is secular or sacred. So, if the highly Socialist-influenced, officially Pro-Choice legal human-killing governing political party (which makes sure all its provincial and national members *reject* the Pro-Life *Foundational Principles of Human Rights and Democracy* identified from History, Science, Logic and Philosophy in this book series) claims it is *not* bigoted against religion, then it should have "Coronavirus Measures" imposed on religious activities which are commensurate with those imposed on secular activities; if it is bigoted, then it should at least be *honest* about it and simply impose an extra tax on Christians and other religious believers for existing and for worshiping, like they do in countries without traditional Western values like religious freedom. But do not dare to dishonestly claim you are "protecting us from the virus" by allowing us to go to fun centers and restaurants with hundreds of others but not allowing us to gather to worship!

Note too, that as expected from *Relativist not Realist ideologues*, all of the "Coronavirus Measures" in any case are developed and upheld in court *while never engaging and just pretending there is no vast and multi-faceted movement of medical professionals against Coronavirus alarmism and against lockdowns. Lockdowns which have never before been medical procedures, but rather prison procedures – so if you feel imprisoned by your government's lockdown policies, you are correct! A vast number of medical professionals and medical scientists who see the typical government Coronavirus Measures as doing far more harm than good have associated in numerous professional groupings including (but not limited to) the signatories of the Great Barrington Declaration of over 55,500 and counting medical scientists and other medical professionals [2nd Printing Update: now 62,119 and counting medical scientists and other medical professionals] who powerfully testify, and are backed up by the publicly available*

CARTESIAN SKEPTICISM

Coronavirus statistics, that oppressive Coronavirus Measures that restrict normal democratic freedoms for the general population are no longer necessary (and only "Focused Protection" for the minority actually vulnerable to the Coronavirus should continue). If the Marxist "Great Reset" piggy-backing on the Pandemic, which is so well served by unmedical lockdowns – and by people getting used to *not being free* like they used to be – was not a goal of so many Relativist and Marxist and globalist ideologues worldwide, the Pandemic would long be over already. It only continues into 2021 [update: now into 2022] because of *Relativism not Realism* in action – anything ideologues do not like and cannot beat otherwise, they just *pretend it does not exist!* Thus, many tens of thousands of qualified medical and scientific voices against oppressive Coronavirus policies are censored and buried by the mainstream media (now intertwined with "Big Tech") which Solzhenitsyn long ago warned us was Relativist, Marxist influenced and taking the "Free West" eventually to totalitarian ends *like these undemocratic restrictions the world now lives under,* with no end in sight as long as Relativist and Marxist-influenced ideologues control information and public opinion through mainstream media and "Big Tech." Whose personnel are hereby given THE INTELLECTUAL HONESTY CHALLENGE as part of the THINKING REVOLUTION, wherein they are challenged to finally start THINKING honestly and logically – challenged to finally get a HUMAN RIGHTS EDUCATION FOR LAST FREE DEMOCRACY and become part of a FREE and prosperous human society built on *(Scientific) Realism not (Skeptical) Relativism* and built on *Equal Human Rights for All Humans.*

But long before the Coronavirus Pandemic, it was already true that sensible judgements cannot be expected from those influenced by Relativism and Marxism. With philosophical *Relativists not Realists* in government long before the Pandemic, it is not even really surprising that in only three weeks in 2017, where this author and Dr. Jordan Peterson lived, the officially Pro-Choice (and effectively Neo-Marxist *Extremist* Left-wing, totalitarian-oriented) government passed laws meaning peaceful Pro-Life Human Rights advocates can be arrested and jailed for speaking verifiable scientific facts about abortion, or doing any kind of advocacy on behalf of *Equal Human Rights for All Humans.* Other jurisdictions copied this law including another Canadian province controlled by Pro-Choice Relativist politicians which passed a similar totalitarian law *in only 8 days,* March 2-10, 2020. Similarly, a Relativist judge told a father where I live that he will go to jail if he speaks verifiable scientific facts to or about his daughter (including calling her his daughter, even though every cell in her body is scientifically, demonstrably female; his daughter who has already been permanently chemically sterilized against her father's will by newfangled unscientific ideology promoted aggressively by Pro-Choice Neo-Marxist *Relativist* (therefore *anti-Realist*) political parties in power. [Update: In a serendipitous example of how we are all in the flow of *Living History* happening all around us, just as I was about to upload to my publisher the first Emergency Edition/Advance Reader Copy in early 2021, I received news that that father *is now in jail* for calling his daughter his daughter and for using accurate pronouns reflective of scientifically verifiable reality about her. The father with sardonic gratefulness wryly commented that at least "The court was gracious enough to say that they could not police my thoughts." [3] My fellow Canadian intellectual for Free Speech, Professor Jordan Peterson, has been proven *exactly right* for standing up and saying in 2016 that the totalitarian Bill C-16 (since made law) he became famous for opposing would precisely

---

[3] See https://thepostmillennial.com/rob-hoogland-canada-prisoner-of-conscience, accessed March 19, 2021.
https://www.breitbart.com/tech/2021/03/18/canadian-man-jailed-after-misgendering-his-daughter/, accessed March 19, 2021.

lead to this kind of absurd and totalitarian restrictions on free speech. A father is in jail just for talking about the scientific fact he for the last 14 years has had a daughter, not a son. But Relativist *subjectivists*, having no grip on any *objective reality*, find it very easy to dishonestly *relabel* anything according to their vacuous *ideology* instead of according to any solid *education.* And when Relativist subjectivists are politicians or judges, they have time and again proven only too willing to use *force of law* to *force into silence* anyone who actually believes in Science and Logic and facts and not in their Relativist ideologies which have nothing to do with facts.

In any case, all of the academic and media and "Big Tech" censorship supporting such abject political stupidity;

disallowing academic research projects that would expose facts about government-approved ideological foolishness;

contrary-to-fact *pretending* that there is *not* a vast amount of highly qualified medical science testimony *against* Coronavirus alarmism and lockdowns, in order to use an unnecessarily ongoing and never-ending "Pandemic State of Emergency" to facilitate the Marxist "Great Reset;"

now even making speaking verifiable Science a crime and politically promoting new forms of the anti-scientific, Skeptical, Atheistic, Relativistic Marxism which has killed more humans than anything else in history –

all this is now happening ultimately because in the 17th Century *Cartesian Skepticism* unhinged Western Philosophy from the previously dominant Aristotelian (and Scholastic) *Realism* which gave the West Logic, Science and Technology. So, continuing the above bulleted list (started in Chapter 4) of the various things which have come into the West through Cartesian Skepticism:

- *Marxism,* which, starting from Atheism (Solzhenitsyn confirms that Atheism is no side feature but is integral to Marxism) is by far the most sophisticated and popular of Atheistic political theories. Marxism is so insidiously, seductively popular that there are still, as Solzhenitsyn noted of the 1920s and 1930s (when Marxists were cannibalizing his beloved Russia and committing the *Holodomor* Genocide of this author's ethnic group), "an enormous number of Western intellectuals" of Atheist/ Marxist/ Communist/ Socialist bent, who "refuse to see communism's crimes" or "try to justify them." These include the Marxists who, to save Marxism from being debunked by the *facts* that Marxism in practice always leads to horrendous and genocidally murderous totalitarian States, developed and continue:

- *Postmodernist philosophy*, which denies the reality of even facts and Science, reviving the most radically skeptical conclusions of Cartesian Skepticism which most (including Descartes himself) had refused to live by. The Postmodernism that keeps Marxism alive tends to often go side-by-side with:
- *Neo-Marxist Identity Politics*, which continues Marx's radical and unrealistic reinterpretation of all history and politics as an inherently adversarial (and therefore toxic to *cooperation* for the Common Good) "class struggle" between those labelled "oppressed" and "privileged," intending to create by any means a seductive Marxist-type egalitarian utopia – undaunted by the *facts* that any type of Marxism has always resulted in oppressive totalitarian States due to Marxism's fundamental flaws, because Identity Politics is deeply rooted in the same radically skeptical and vacuous philosophical origins as

solipsism, which ultimately *denies or doubts Reality as we all daily experience it even exists.*
- *Neo-Marxist "Cancel Culture,"* which continues classic Marxism's *Skeptical Relativism not Scientific Realism* by wherever possible erasing and silencing ("cancelling" or censoring) voices, *even expert scientific voices*, against their ideological agendas, *just like all Marxist states controlled society by controlling which voices are heard.*
- On the (only somewhat) more positive side, the stream of Western Philosophy emanating from Cartesian Skepticism includes *Existentialism*, which tries to "make the best of" the radical uncertainty dominating Western Philosophy since Descartes, by bravely, courageously facing the (since Descartes) apparently meaningless universe which we cannot even be sure really exists outside of our own minds, taking responsibility for our own actions as we seek to apply some kind of meaning to our human lives. Existentialism nominally accepts the reality of other minds than one's own (but cannot be certain about this). Taking responsibility for our own actions is, of course, very mature and good (and something Marxism never does – Marxism always blames someone else for "oppressing" us, fomenting resentment and hatred which Marxism intends to spill over into bloody revolution to overturn the existing government, so that a Marxist egalitarian utopia can be attempted . . . even though every attempt in history has resulted in millions of murders in oppressive totalitarian States). Unfortunately, because Existentialism assumes the *radical* not *reasonable* doubts inherent in Cartesian Skepticism, and thus, is ultimately unsure of any

objective reality, Existentialist individuals *subjectively* and individually apply meaning to life, meaning which can have widely divergent political consequences for other humans (who may or may not even exist, in Modern Philosophy which started with Cartesian Skepticism. A "successful" Existentialist life is one that avoids both solipsism and suicide by assigning meaning to an otherwise meaningless universe and takes responsibility for one's actions while doing so). Kierkegaard, generally recognized as the first Existentialist, gave meaning to his life in the face of the radical doubts ultimately unleashed by Cartesian Skepticism by choosing to take the "leap of faith" required to embrace Christianity. This kind of way around radical skepticism *in faith* works well in practice for one's self and other humans, because Christianity is the source of *The Foundational Principles of Human Rights and Democracy* (Descartes himself had remained devoutly Christian to stay sane). But Atheist (and thus Moral Relativist) Existentialist Nietzsche despised what he called the "slave morality" of Christianity; he despised not only Marxist Socialism but also Democracy (built on Christian principles) for promoting (in different ways) human equality (though in Marxism, humans are equal but not precious, which is why so many get murdered in Marxist States). Nietzsche's way of assigning meaning to the otherwise meaningless and lonely existence left by the radical skepticism inherent in Modern Philosophy since Descartes was to (like a true Atheist Moral Relativist) *create one's own morality*, with a "will to power." Nietzsche's thought, which despised human equality in favor of elitism of the "exceptional" (like himself, of course), ultimately influenced Hitler and Nazism. Brilliant Nietzsche, much more intellectually honest than his fellow German Atheist Marx, perhaps moreso than some Existentialists was *tormented* by the radical skepticism inherent in Modern Philosophy since Descartes, which naturally leads to solipsism or Nihilism. The Merriam Webster Dictionary defines Nihilism as "a viewpoint that traditional values and beliefs are unfounded and that existence is senseless and useless. *Nihilism is a condition in which all ultimate values lose their value.*" Nihilist Nietzsche in his book *The Gay Science* has a character called "the Madman" declare "God is dead! God remains dead! And we have killed Him! How shall we comfort ourselves, we who are the biggest murderers of all?" It seems Atheist Nietzsche could find no comfort for his "Existentialist Angst" and, although he (like a successful Existentialist) avoided solipsism and suicide, he still actually spent the last 11 years of his life in an insane asylum – in a way becoming himself "the Madman" who proclaimed "God is Dead." And sadly, his thought becoming more popular after his death, his biggest effect on history was first:

influencing the Nazis (his influence on the Nazis was specifically mentioned at the Nuremberg War Crimes Trials of the Nazis) and second:

his "God is dead" phrase being popularized in the New York Times in the 1960s, this phrase has since been used axiomatically by Atheists whose (frequently Marxist!) leanings are among the biggest threats to Free Democracy which is built on Christian principles.

Frenchman Jean-Paul Sartre too, like Nietzsche, was an Atheist Existentialist whose personal, "subjective" attempt to bring meaning to an "objectively" meaningless existence without any objective certainty at all (thanks to Cartesian Skepticism) did more to harm humans, because he actually embraced and promoted Marxism, which has killed more humans than anything else in history. Existentialism's emphasis on "taking personal responsibility" in Sartre perhaps softened the typical Marxist approach of never taking personal responsibility but blaming others for your misfortunes, violently overthrowing whatever "privileged" class "oppresses" you in order to initiate a Marxist State. So, Sartre never joined a Marxist, Communist party. But still Sartre (like all the "enormous number" of Western Marxists Solzhenitsyn criticized for this) *hid*, *made excuses for* and *tried to justify* all the Marxist Soviet Union's atrocities. Sartre even actually attacked later Soviet Leader Khrushchev's refreshing candor in admitting and condemning the worst Soviet Marxist atrocities under former Soviet Marxist Leader Josef Stalin - because telling the truth about Marxism is bad for Marxism (Solzhenitsyn, who exposed Marxism's ideological and practical evil in *The Gulgag Archipelago*, had as a motto "one word of truth outweighs the whole world"). Sartre's French Marxist writings were inspirational for the Khmer Rouge (Communist Party of Kampuchea) under Pol Pot in Cambodia, who first studied in Paris, where his French Marxist professors encouraged his plan to initiate a "Marxist utopia" in Cambodia, which (because Marxism never works) resulted in the deaths of one quarter of Cambodia's population through mass starvation and genocides against Cambodia's ethnic minorities (both recalling the earlier *Holodomor* ["Murder by Starvation"] genocide through enforced starvation against this author's ethnic heritage in the Marxist USSR). Sartre's contemporary and erstwhile friend Albert Camus is also known as an Existentialist, a categorization he himself denied, because instead of trying to subjectively and responsibly assign meaning to one's meaningless existence in a meaningless universe as Existentialists do, Camus instead advocated giving in to or *embracing the absurdity of such existence,* in:

- The philosophy of *Absurdism*, which, deeply rooted in the radical expression of Cartesian Skepticism which has been a powerful undercurrent of Western philosophy since Descartes' 17th Century error, highlights and embraces the supposed absurd incongruity between the human drive to search for meaning in life, and the supposed inability of humans to find any satisfactory meaning in a universe which (since the Cartesian Split) is presumed meaningless, purposeless, irrational and chaotic, or at least unknowable to be otherwise.

But, this author contends, there is no need to so give in to the alleged "absurdity of human life," nor any need to try to wiggle out of the demented solipsism, denying or doubting Reality itself outside one's own mind, which is the logical end of Cartesian Skepticism, whether by the "Cartesian Circle" Descartes himself used, or by Existentialism's brave facing of the meaningless and uncertain universe left by Cartesian Skepticism (with very mixed political results for human safety coming out of Existentialist philosophers). There is no need to "try to make the best of an ultimately uncertain and meaningless existence" as Existentialism does, because such doubts are *radical* not *reasonable* doubts, and there is good *reason* to return to the previous dominant stream in Western Philosophy (which scientists never stopped operating within) which accepts our *common human experience of the universe* (without which you could not even read this book, nor understand it) as *real.* Ancient Aristotelian Realism *ignores Modern Cartesian Skepticism* and all the vast doubts it has brought about in Modern Philosophy since the 17th Century, and just goes on as before Modern Philosophy, *successfully plugging away* at gradually unravelling the secrets of the material universe humans live in through Science; and ingeniously applying what the Pure Sciences discover in the Applied and Industrial Sciences including *Technology.* The fact that Science works at all, and provides us with amazing new technologies previously undreamed of, is a powerful testament to the veracity of the Aristotelian Realism which Cartesian Skepticism denies or unreasonably doubts...

. . . by happy accident (or Providence) this author shortly before this Emergency Edition's rushed publication (to help save Free Democracy from Relativists) came across the 1957 book *An Introduction to Philosophy: Perennial Principles of the Classical Realist Tradition* by Daniel. J. Sullivan. Glancing through, it appears to be an excellent text on Realism. Written before the West abandoned Traditional Western Values in the 1960s and replaced *The Foundational Principles of Human Rights and Democracy* (Judeo-Christian in origin) with Atheist Relativism and Moral Relativism, as the West's "guiding principles for public policy" – ultimately resulting in the current 'Creeping Totalitarianism' now accelerating towards the totalitarian end of the Free West which Solzhenitsyn warned the West was coming due to the West's embracing Relativist, Atheist, Marxist principles. Sullivan's text furnishes these thoughts on Descartes' subjectivism which almost four centuries ago

CARTESIAN SKEPTICISM

unleashed the false thinking now undermining Human Rights and freedoms globally:

[Descartes'] position is called subjectivism because it is based on the consciousness of the thinking subject, making the objects of knowledge a part of the thinking subject himself, his ideas, his feelings and so forth, so that there is no objective, external test of truth.

Descartes, when he demanded proof for the existence of the outside world, started a false problem which gave rise in modern philosophy to innumerable errors: a false problem because the question is asked in such a way that no answer is possible ... We do not invent, or create the existences which form the field of our knowledge. We <u>discover</u> these existences, and there is no possible way of knowing what has, in fact, been given existence other than to discover it ... For the philosopher to ask proof of the actual existence of contingent things, including his own existence, is to betray [to not accept] the evidence of the fundamental intuition of his senses and intellect. It is to ask proof for what does not need proof, for what indeed cannot be proved, since it is prior to proof and implied in all demonstration.

"The one reason why we state that we exist and that London is in England is because reality is that way. Being is the lord of the intellect and whenever we make a judgement that we know is true and certain, it is because being is so presented to the intellect that reality determines, forces and constrains us to consent to it. There can be no turning back at this point because in the field of knowledge-content the intellect is the servant, reality the master, and it is reality that dictates to the intellect, not vice-versa."

... We may conclude by affirming that when the subjectivist asks you to prove the existence of the world of bodies, he is refusing to accept the evidence in the only place where it can be found—in the world of bodies itself. In fact, this is the only conceivable place where it can be found, since it is a contingent existence not made by us or brought into existence by our thought. The arbitrary refusal of the subjectivist to accept the evidence in the only place where it can be found

precludes beforehand the possibility of any answer, as in the classical example of a man who asks what numbers make up twelve, but precludes you from using twice six, or three times four, or twelve times one. [A classical example from Aristotle's mentor Plato]

Descartes' (temporary for him) radically skeptical subjectivism encapsulated in the error "I think, *therefore* I am" absurdly tried to make his own intellect and comprehension dictate what is real, when in fact (prior, and independent) *reality* dictates to the intellect (through the senses) the *evidence* of reality. What is real is *evident* to us, through our senses, which is why all of us individual human subjects gathered around the same breakfast table see (that is, we *experience* the *evidence* of through our sense of sight) the same orange on the table. The orange by its very existence makes *evident* its reality upon us through our senses. And if you, a subjectivist and relativist around the table, deny the orange is real, deny the *evidence* of the orange's existence the only place it can be found (through your senses), even though you see it just like the rest of us around the table do – no matter how strenuously you philosophically deny the real existence of the orange, the concrete, commonly experienced *reality* of *Reality* means you simply cannot prevent yourself from also experiencing the *evidence* of the orange's real existence through the rest of your senses (hearing, touch, taste and smell) when I whip the orange in your face and you hear me say "silly Skeptic Relativist, deny this!" As this author has stated elsewhere, the *reality* of *Reality* imposes or forces itself upon each of us individual human subjects with *common consistency* through our *common human senses* which we *reasonably* accept as putting us more or less directly in contact with a really existing universe of Reality external to and independent of our minds. A real universe studied as *real* by *really existing* (pure) scientists who are, by accepting this universe's *reality* and closely examining it, able to *discover* ever-new things about Reality they did not invent, but which give other (applied) scientists new and deeper information about the universe they can creatively use to invent new technology ... all based on Realism not Relativism. All this fruitfulness from accepting the (common, sensory) *evidence* that the universe is real means it is eminently reasonable to accept the universe is real. It is in fact unreasonable – and literally dangerous – to *not* so accept the evidence of external reality the only place it may be found, through our senses. No matter how strenuously you skeptics and relativists deny the existence of the Mack truck sliding out-of-control towards you on its side, you *will* get squashed like a bug if you unreasonably take no steps to avoid it because you doubt its real existence independent of your own mind (a mind physically associated with a brain which may end up spread over the Mack truck's windshield...). It is *radical not reasonable* skepticism, and intellectual dishonesty, to keep denying all the sensory evidence of the external reality we individual humans all commonly experience daily and cannot get out of contact with *unless we literally go insane* and so become irrelevant to the external world we deny. No sane person lives like this, nor can skeptics and relativists survive long (outside of a mental institution where competent *realists* look after the safety of deranged *skeptics*). It is ultimately *hypocritical* (and politically dangerous for everyone else) for you to survive every day only by acting according to the evidence that Reality is real from the only place that evidence comes – your senses – but then make your political philosophy and undertake political actions based on radical skepticism and relativism which *radically doubt or deny reality*, like Marxists and all other Moral Relativists do.

Daniel J. Sullivan's book *An Introduction to Philosophy: Perennial Principles of The Classical Realist Tradition* also provides a response to the skeptic, which also in the end urges the skeptic to reasonably abandon his or her philosophical skepticism for the sake of intellectual honesty and consistency, also noting (like Aristotle noted of his critics millennia ago) that it is actually impossible to live consistently as a skeptic. The untrained human default is to live (and not die) according to Common Sense which unconsciously, implicitly grasps the essence of *Reality* articulated scientifically by *Realism* anyway. So one might as well choose to live consciously by the underlying philosophical worldview of *Realism* that can (unlike Skepticism and Relativism) be *realistically* (and fruitfully!) lived:

To demonstrate the error of skepticism to the skeptic is impossible because the skeptic refuses to accept the principles which make demonstration possible ... It is not necessary to question the sincerity of the person who calls himself a skeptic but it is legitimate to remind him of the difference between a verbal [claimed] doubt and of what is implied by real doubt. Real doubt paralyzes activity. If you had a <u>real</u> doubt whether or not your food was poisoned you would not eat it. If you had a <u>real</u> doubt of the safety of the elevator you would walk. If you had a <u>real</u> doubt doubt of the destination of your train, you would get out and ask. Of course, if you had a <u>real</u> doubt of everything you would doubt the very existence of the food, of the elevator, of the train. You would also doubt, <u>really</u> doubt, the existence of other people, of your own past, of the immediate future. If a person <u>really</u> doubted all the evidence of his senses and intellect, he would be able only to lift his little finger, as Aristotle puts it. The absolute skeptic is reduced, in short, to the existence of a vegetable. This is one check, then, that can be made against the absolute skeptic. Does he really act as though he had a real doubt of everything? For if someone asserts a philosophical position as true, it is legitimate to ask whether he acts in accordance with his asserted philosophy.

Cartesian Skepticism

In this case, this author posits, since it is impossible to live a human life at all as a consistent skeptic or relativist, then *get real*! Those who hold Pro-Choice or Marxist or other Morally Relativist philosophical and political positions have positions which are built upon the erroneous and absurd *radical doubt or denial of reality itself* inherent in philosophical Skepticism and Relativism. Skepticism and Relativism which are *opposed* to the philosophical *Realism* which accords with the innate human gift of Common Sense that daily *keeps us alive* and which puts us daily into *contact with reality*. Skepticism and Relativism which are *opposed* to the philosophical *Realism* which, building on (innate and unconscious) Common Sense and making it scientific, critical, conscious, gives us Science, Logic, and Technology. And gives us a *realistic* philosophical framework within which to fruitfully live our human lives. This book series, even in this unedited first "Emergency Edition" form which is published early to combat the speeding freight-train of once 'creeping' totalitarianism *now accelerating fast towards free democracy's destruction in the West,* has already amply demonstrated from Human Rights History just how insidiously dangerous Pro-Choice and Marxist and other philosophically Relativistic positions are, and how necessary to ongoing human safety and freedom are *The Foundational Principles of Human Rights and Democracy*, which are of course built on philosophical *Realism*, thus having a good grip on *Reality* and according with Common Sense!

. . . How does all the above History of Philosophy and above philosophical considerations affect current Western and world politics? Both the *Realistic* and the *Radically Skeptical and Relativistic* streams of Philosophy, which are entirely incompatible with each other, have been concurrently *strongly* influential in Western and world society and culture for centuries now. Meaning most people, influenced by both streams, have unconsciously, gradually, gravitated towards and more or less settled *on one or the other* as their "dominant" underlying worldview concerning their (usually subconscious) assumptions about the big "First Order Questions" of the nature and meaning of the material universe we humans commonly perceive and daily interact with – and humanity's place and purpose (and our own individual place and purpose) within that universe. Ultimately resulting in a *polarized*, bifurcated current Western politics, rooted ultimately in polarized, fundamentally incompatible, underlying fundamental philosophical assumptions about the universe and about humanity. Of course this has a major affect on whether we accept the legal killing of humans, which is the central topic of the author's book *Pro-Life Equals Pro-Democracy* in which this discussion was first printed! So naturally, the political polarization largely falls along the lines that those who are strongly *for* the legal killing of humans by abortion, or who vote for political parties now "officially Pro-Choice" (parties which now often no longer even accept members who are not Pro-Choice; and which "purge" from their ranks "old guard" party members who are still Pro-Life), tend to be primarily (at least unconsciously) *philosophical relativists*. They tend to be primarily (at least unconsciously) *philosophical realists,* those who are Pro-Life (easily accepting the *scientific reality* that preborn humans are humans, *without trying to wiggle out of this reality like relativist Pro-Choice bigots do*), or who vote for political parties which – though too often too terrified of Marxist-influenced Mainstream Media to be officially Pro-Life – yet are still "big tent" and freethinking enough to accept into their party Pro-Lifers with their Traditional Western Pro-Life Family Values that Free Democracy is historically and logically built on . . .

Since most people have not consciously been taught nor learned the above *History of Ideas,* most people have not consciously thought through their underlying philosophical options, nor have most people consciously *chosen* a basic philosophical worldview. Thus, most people have just unconsciously *absorbed* various, and not necessarily consistent, *assumptions* about the basic nature of the universe and the nature and meaning of human life, from their environment, and from whatever level and type of education they have had. Which may have been a good education based on established facts of Science and History, including the History of Philosophy so they might make some form of conscious judgement about their philosophical options; or a bad education that imparts *ideology* instead of genuine *education*, as that spread by the Marxists who developed Postmodernist philosophy to protect Marxism from the facts that Marxism never works in practice. The Sullivan quote above notes that faulty education like this, now all too common in Western universities (as Solzhenitsyn warned us), can actually mentally *impair* people from fully accessing the Common Sense, humanity's innate gift that puts humans in contact with *reality*, which accords with the philosophical Realism which grounds Science, Logic, and Technology.

The current political bifurcation of society which makes it so hard to find common ground is ultimately rooted in the fact that the relative strength or weakness of one's firmly Realistic or Radically Skeptical influences and assumptions will incline each person to gravitate to either the Realistic or the Skeptical/Relativistic as their "general worldview," which will influence their politics. And chances are many people have some inconsistent and incompatible assumptions that they absorbed and live according to in different areas of their lives – including some silly assumptions they would never choose consciously, and for good reason, which is why THE THINKING REVOLUTION proclaimed in this book is so important, so that most people can at last *consciously identify* and live by a *consistent* underlying philosophical worldview – which will greatly help resolve the current political bifurcation and division of society which is ultimately rooted in opposing and incompatible philosophical views of the universe and human life as a whole.

CHAPTER 6
PROFESSOR STEPHEN HICKS, AUTHOR OF *EXPLAINING POSTMODERNISM: SKEPTICISM AND SOCIALISM FROM ROUSSEAU TO FOUCAULT*, EXPLAINS WHY & HOW EACH NEW GENERATION OF PROGRESSIVE SOCIALIST POSTMODERNIST PROFESSORS HAS LESS INTELLECTUAL CAPACITY AND LESS INTELLECTUAL HONESTY WITH WHICH TO TRAIN THE NEXT GENERATION AFTER THEM – *FOR A PROGRESSIVE DEVOLUTION OF INTELLECTUAL QUALITY IN UNIVERSITIES*

> *"One world, one mankind cannot exist in the face of ... two scales of values: We shall be torn apart by this disparity of rhythm, this disparity of vibrations."*
> — *Aleksandr Solzhenitsyn*

Yes, I am here making a value judgement that a Realistic education is good, and a Skeptical education is bad, but that judgement is made based on my *knowing* the History of Ideas/History of Philosophy, and *knowing* the History of World Politics so I can see how the former has affected the latter. Most Pro-Choice, Neo-Marxist Identity Politics "Cancel Culture" ideologues and "social justice warriors" have neither a broad understanding of Philosophy nor History (nor Science, nor Logic . . .)

In fact, Professor Stephen Hicks, author of *Explaining Postmodernism: Skepticism and Socialism from Rousseau to Foucault*, having studied the origins and current state of Postmodernism, notes that the current (2nd/3rd generation) of Postmodernists is of lower intellectual quality. Naturally, since their skeptical ideology means they have never had the rigorous education the first generation had before they came to their erroneous conclusions.

> *"Nothing worthy can be built on a neglect of higher meanings and on a relativistic view of concepts and culture as a whole."*
> *"The generation now coming out of Western schools is unable to distinguish good from bad. Even those words are unacceptable. This results in impaired thinking ability."*
> *". . . We have arrived at an intellectual chaos."*
> — *Aleksandr Solzhenitsyn*

Progressive Devolution of Intellectual Quality

The first generation of Postmodernists, well-educated themselves but becoming skeptical and relativistic, absurdly concluded there is no objective reality – so they do not need to take science, logic, rationality, nor the quest for objectivity seriously. So, their students *start off* not even taking science, logic, rationality, nor the quest for objectivity seriously. So, in Western universities, as Solzhenitsyn warned of the dangers of Relativism, you end up with Ph.D.s who do not even take science, logic, rationality, nor the quest for objectivity seriously. Ph.D.s who have not developed higher order thinking skill-sets themselves, who emphasize *feelings* instead of *thinking*; and *opinions* instead of *facts* (facts which they absurdly think do not exist or cannot be known anyways). Postmodernist philosophy means new professors promote emotionalism and (brainless) political activism instead of thinking (which the professors do not know how to do very well themselves). These next generation professors of less intellectual capacity and less intellectual honesty train the next generation after them for *a progressive devolution of intellectual quality*. We are seeing the result of radically skeptical Postmodernist philosophy over a few generations, and suffering the results in politicians who, because of being exposed to or explicitly trained in Postmodernist philosophy in universities, have, in a more vernacular term, "mush for brains." We are seeing and suffering the political activism of "social justice warriors" and politicians inspired and guided by those with high intellectual dishonesty and/or "mush for brains."

A big danger Professor Stephen Hicks notes is that Postmodernist professors who do not believe in any objective truth, only subjective opinion, are spreading their subjective opinions to their students *instead of training them to think for themselves,* instead of making sure they know the previous generations of thought, analyze them and make their own decisions as free thinkers. So, like Aleksandr

Solzhenitsyn noticed and warned the West decades ago but the West did not listen, *the universities are becoming less and less truly educational*, and less and less relevant to real life – except for how relevant to real life it is that supposedly university-educated people (including politicians) now spout ultimately anti-democratic (and anti-scientific) relativistic ideologies (including but not limited to legal human-killing Pro-Choice ideology and Neo-Marxist Identity Politics with its "Cancel Culture") which endanger both society and now Science and scholarship itself . . .

. . . So, if you claim that the Radically Skeptical stream of Philosophy is superior to or more correct than the Realistic stream of Philosophy, that means that deep down, in your unconsciously assumed philosophical worldview, you really do not know for certain that anything outside of your own mind even exists. That means, if you are correct, you therefore must have "just made up" this author, and your iPhone, or else you were deceived by some "evil demon" (as Descartes postulated) with nothing better to do than *deceive* you into sensing an objective reality with authors and iPhones, when "in fact" nothing outside your mind really exists. So, if you are correct that the Radically Skeptical stream of Philosophy is more accurate than Philosophical Realism which assumes the universe Science studies actually exists, then it ultimately *cannot really matter to you* what happens in World Politics, since to you none of that world/universe external to and independent of your mind actually exists anyway. So, *please get the hell out of politics.* Politics cannot actually matter to you if the world that engages in politics is not actually real, so please, on the chance that the rest of us actually exist, like we think we do, please, please get the hell out of politics. *Real people* have already died in the tens of millions from deep-down radical skeptic anti-scientific Pro-Choicers and Neo-Marxist Identity Politics "Cancel Culture" ideologues like you being politically active and trying to brainlessly make the "Red Square peg" of Marxism fit into the "round hole" of Reality, when it just does not fit. In the *Real World* all humans commonly perceive but which the rest of us (unlike you radical skeptics) assume is *real*, peaceful Human Rights advocates like this author can now be arrested and jailed for saying "killing humans is wrong because Human Rights are for All Humans" under totalitarian laws passed by intellectually dishonest (or "ideologically lobotomized") Pro-Choice legal human-killing Identity Politics ideologues like yourself, with an underlying radically skeptical *lack of grip on reality* and this has to stop. *Real people* will thank you for stopping, and you have plenty of good reason for doing so, as in the further *pensées* below . . .

♦

. . . Skeptics grossly overstate the importance of the *limitations* of our human senses . . . The very limitations of our human senses are accounted for by Aristotelian Realism and the Scientific Method. As we observe discrepancies in our observations, we make new scientific theories to account for the data. We invent new procedures and new scientific instruments for collecting more data, and/or better quality data, all from *TRUSTING* our human senses and our observations of the Natural Universe, in order to come up with an even better scientific theory that better approximates objective reality. Yes, it is an approximation, but yes, we can learn more about it, which is why Science continues and gets more and more detailed and precise – according to Aristotelian Realist Principles not Cartesian Skeptical ones . . . all of the necessary assumptions of Science – and of Common Sense – are all inherited from or rooted in the Realist tradition back through Saint Thomas Aquinas and the Scholastic Tradition, all the way back to Aristotle . . . even the possibility of the occasional need for a new paradigm or theory to account for more, better observational data in the future of scientific enquiry is part of the Pure Sciences and the Modern Scientific Method as developed within the Scholastic (and Thomist) philosophical tradition in the European universities, firmly grounded in Aristotelian Realism ...

... Atheism and Secularism are both ultimately and fundamentally *religious* philosophical positions with clear perspectives on "First Order Questions" (or "religious questions") of the nature of the universe and the meaning of human life – and how public political policy should be guided. Typically, Atheists and Secularists ridiculously claim that traditional theistic and (in the West) Judeo-Christian religious perspectives and values should have "no influence in the public sphere," even though it is Biblical, Judeo-Christian religious principles which include and uphold *The Foundational Principles of Human Rights and Democracy*, and even though the lack of these Judeo-Christian principles in all Atheist (usually Marxist) States has been direct cause of horrendous atrocities, and murders and genocides killing millions of humans. The typical Atheist and Secularist views on the big "First Order" questions, as shown in this author's books, are completely devoid of any significant Human Rights Education; and are based in *ignorance* of rather than any *knowledge* of the Human Rights History, the Science and Logic (and the History of Science and Logic) which helps identify *The Foundational Principles of Human Rights and Democracy . . . But ...*

... The (devout Christian) scientists (Both Catholic, like Galileo, and Protestant, like Newton) who developed the Scientific Method, by doing so made up for the major weakness in Aristotle. Aristotle's articulations of the First Principles of Being or First Principles of Existence remain the solid foundation of all logic and science . . . However, when it came to articulating specific scientific theories to account for observed data, since Aristotle (grounded by Realism) basically started the entire endeavor of Science, he started with no collected scientific data at all, so of course not all of his theories to account for the (extremely limited) data he had access to were correct, we now know. But we know it *because* the scientific *process* Aristotle started makes detailed observations of Nature and theorizes about the data, abandoning older theories when more, newer, better data becomes available and reveals weaknesses in the older theories, requiring newer better theories be formulated to account for more and superior data. Theories which themselves will be modified or abandoned in the future, when more or better data is available. It would be silly to criticize Aristotle for being millennia later proven *wrong* about some of his specific biological theories in ancient times, when, unlike today's scientists, he had *no* collected data nor past thoughtful theorization to ground his initial scientific theories upon. But he gave us Science itself – including Science's ability to observe and correct weaknesses in past theories when new data becomes available. Aristotle's *First Principles of Being/Existence* – and of Science which studies existence – were and are rock-solid. But Aristotle, as effectively the very first Scientist of course did not start off with millennia of already-gathered scientific observations and insight like today's scientists do, "standing on the shoulders of giants" who have gone before them, as Sir Isaac Newton said. Newton who, with all the other (devoutly Christian) founders of Modern Science in the Scientific Revolution, were at last able to identify and overcome the one major weakness of Aristotle. Particularly, Aristotle lacked the later-developed Scientific Method. Aristotle's Science included little or no "experimentation" as we know it today; but only detailed observations of nature and rudimentary deeper investigations of nature like dissecting animals to "look and observe what is inside" as part of Aristotle's beginning the Science of Biology . . .

CHAPTER 7
FIRST ORDER QUESTIONS AND WORLDVIEW: WHY IS THERE SOMETHING RATHER THAN NOTHING? IS YOUR WORLDVIEW FUNDAMENTALLY REALIST (AND SCIENTIFIC) OR (LIKE MARXISM'S) RADICALLY SKEPTICAL (THAT IS, OUT OF TOUCH WITH OR DENYING REALITY). YOUR POLITICS FOLLOWS SUIT

What it comes down to is that in attempting to answer deep First Order questions about the nature of existence, such as "where did the universe come from?" and "Why is there something and not nothing?," whether you are Atheist or Christian or anything in between, you are ultimately forced to assume that *something* has simply always existed or by its nature simply *cannot not exist*, whatever that *something* is. If to answer the question "where did the universe come from" you posit that the universe we humans experience our whole lives in was created and/or ordered by some superior being or god or gods (Science Fiction humorist Douglas Adams writes "The Jatravartid People of Viltvodle Six firmly believe that the entire universe was sneezed out of the nose of a being called The Great Green Arkleseizure"). This invites the obvious question, where did that superior being/god or gods/arkleseizure come from? With this kind of answer it is easy to fall into an absurd infinite regression which just begs the question or avoids the issue of the ultimate foundations of existence (the world was created by this which was created by that which was created by ... *ad infinitum*).

To avoid infinite regression (and to avoid the demented *solipsism* which denies any existence outside of your own mind, in which case you may as well not bother with anything political at all because your mind just made up me and my book and any political parties you could vote for), and to give a serious answer to the question "where did the universe/existence as we know it come from," we in the end have to accept that *something* is pre-existent, *something* has just always existed or cannot not exist.

Just what is that *something*? Only two real options are forthcoming: Either *matter* (the material substance of which the physical universe that daily confronts us is made) is that which has simply always existed and cannot not exist; or *God* is that which has simply always existed and cannot not exist. Pantheism attempts to equate the two, suggesting that ultimately the material universe and everything in it (the planets and stars, any proposed intermediate pantheon of gods, your body and brain, the table you are sitting in, the air you breathe and the food you just ate) is God.

So, (unless he is a lonely solipsist who is only certain his own mind exists), the Atheist must ultimately choose to believe in *matter* as that which has simply always existed and cannot not exist. There is "stuff" or material, matter, which daily confronts our human senses with the physical existence of our planet, our bodies, the air we breathe. The Atheist, who believes in no God superior to or beyond the physical universe, ultimately must accept this *matter* as pre-existent, always just existing. But the Atheist cannot account for (nor predict from Atheist principles and assumptions) the supremely intricate and marvelous *order* of the physical universe, which is why Atheists had nothing whatsoever to do with the founding of Modern Science and the Modern Scientific Method. The Pantheist too, who just calls the material universe God, likewise cannot account for nor predict the wonderfully delicate and intricate order of the material universe, which is an *ordered cosmos* and not a *random chaos*. Which is why Modern Science never developed where Pantheistic (or Atheistic) religious conceptions of the universe of existence hold sway.

But the Christian (or Jew) is informed by the Judeo-Christian Bible that the material universe we humans live our whole lives in was both created and ordered by the pre-existent, intelligent and personal God who "in the beginning" of the created universe of space-time *already existed.* The Bible's first words are "In the beginning, God created the heavens and the earth" [that is, the universe] (Genesis 1:1). God's constant and unending, eternal (timeless) existence is just assumed while describing the beginning and ordered fashioning of the material universe of space and time and matter which humans live in (note Modern Physics confirms the Bible's presentation of time itself as part of the created order of the universe, which therefore God's existence is not subject to, but is Eternal or timeless). God later in the Bible reveals Himself as "I AM," and the Bible's Covenant Name for God is derived from the Hebrew for the verb "To Be," by name thus establishing God as "He who exists;" Being itself, the Absolute Being/Existence on whom all other ("contingent") being (including the created universe) depends for its existence - and for its intricate *order*.

The second verse of the Bible (Genesis 1:2) indicates that the created universe was initially "formless," and proceeds to poetically describe (in ways the Bible's non-scientific original readers could understand) God giving *form* and *order* to that initially "formless" or chaotic matter of the created universe. The Christian (or Jew) accepts *God* instead of mere formless matter as *that which has simply always existed and cannot not exist.* In doing so, the Christian (or Jew) both accounts for the universe's order and in fact predicts that the created material universe must be an *ordered cosmos*, not a *random* and undirected *chaos.* Thus, the Christian, the Jew, and those influenced by Biblical Judaism and Christianity are motivated to look for *patterns* of order, the signs of an *ordering intelligence or designer*, when looking at nature. In particular, the Socratic School Greeks who well knew the Jewish Bible/Christian Old Testament because they respected the older Hebrew/Jewish culture's *Wisdom* (Biblical Jewish King Solomon's wisdom was legendary), got from the earlier Judeo-Christian Scriptures their key notion that the universe of Nature is an *ordered cosmos* and NOT a *random chaos* - and for this reason they started looking at nature for discernible patterns of *intelligent order* and found them, becoming the earliest recognized scientists (Aristotle articulating the *First Principles of Being/Existence* which are foundational to all Western Logic and Science).

Aristotle's First Principles of Being describe the fundamental orderliness (not randomness) of the universe. Aristotle noted in his day that people who disagreed with him were forced by the (ordered and structured) nature of *Reality*, forced by the very nature of the universe to behave *as if he was right* anyway. As indeed Atheists and

First Order Questions and Worldview

Postmodernists today, if they want to live and not die stupidly, are still forced to behave as if the universe is highly structured and (intelligently) ordered, no matter how much they try to claim the universe and human life is an (ultimately meaningless) product of undirected, random chance. Which is an Atheistic belief which has justified all manner of atrocities, such as the *Holodomor* Genocide perpetrated by the Atheist Soviets upon my Ukrainian ethnic group. If human beings are ultimately just random sacks of bio-chemicals, then it truly does not matter how one random sack of chemicals treats another, and morality is indeed *relative*, as Atheists claim. Moral relativists of course are left with no mentally consistent way of saying that Hitler or Stalin or Mao – influenced by German Atheist philosophers Friedrich Nietzsche or Karl Marx – were absolutely *wrong* to kill many millions of humans as they each attempted to "make the world a better place" according to their own estimation, or "creating their own morality," as Nietzsche advocated, without reference to the (Judeo-Christian) Traditional Western Values which underlie all Human Rights and Democratic Freedoms.

The Judeo-Christian passionate and academic search for Truth in all its forms led to Alexander the Great (who studied under Aristotle) putting the Jews in charge of the great Library at Alexandria in Egypt (one of the great cities Alexander named after himself). Both Alexandria in Egypt and Antioch in Syria would house early great Christian schools of higher learning, and the modern university system itself literally grew out of the medieval Christian cathedral schools. At the Christian universities of Christian Europe (and only there) the modern Pure Sciences and Modern Scientific Method were born - developed by centuries of Christians (Catholic and later Protestant as well) working from a Biblical worldview and Biblical *First Principles* of the universe as an intelligently designed, *ordered cosmos*, not a random and undirected, chaotic universe. In every century from the 11th to the 20th, Catholic Christian priests were among the greatest scientists on the cutting edge of scientific discovery, often founding whole branches of the Natural Sciences. A Catholic Christian priest (the Reverend Monsignor Georges Lemaître) was even the co-founder of the 20th Century Big Bang Theory which still dominates the scientific field of Cosmology. So, next time you hear an Atheist say that Atheism has anything at all to do with Science, or claim that Christian religious faith is somehow against or incompatible with Science, remember that such Atheists are just intellectually dishonest people spouting their gross ignorance and lack of education. So uneducated and dishonest they are also either clueless about, or deceptively hiding, the fact that Atheists like them running governments have consistently created most of the most horrific and oppressive and murderous totalitarian States of all history. Such as Atheist Soviet Russia, which was first to legalize abortion and thereby legally eradicate the *Inherent Human Right to Live* which is essential to Human Rights and freedoms (before legalizing the genocide of an estimated 7-10 million of this author's ethnic group). One quarter of Cambodia died under Atheist Marxist policies, and atrocities abound in every Atheist Marxist State, which typically have legal abortion and do not believe *killing humans is wrong*. You have to *not know a lot* to consciously choose an Atheist and/or a Pro-Choice abortion position. That is why this author, to save Human Rights and Free Democracy for my self (now subject to arrest and jail in my country just for saying *killing humans is wrong*); and for my own children and grandchildren and everyone else's, has developed (and is still developing) this HUMAN RIGHTS EDUCATION FOR LASTING FREE DEMOCRACY, and has proclaimed THE THINKING REVOLUTION in my first professionally published book, *Pro-Life Equals Pro-Democracy* (unedited as it is because I cannot think and write near as fast as today's Pro-Choice, Neo-Marxist

FIRST ORDER QUESTIONS AND WORLDVIEW

Identity Politics "Cancel Culture" politicians can unthinkingly "cancel" Free Speech and dismantle Democracy without a clue what they are doing).

This author is happy to have intelligent discussion with intellectually honest Atheists who may be Atheist simply due to *ignorance* of many of the facts collected in this author's HUMAN RIGHTS EDUCATION FOR LASTING FREE DEMOCRACY book series. More and more knowledgeable and honest Atheists, in response to current accelerating attacks on Freedom of Speech and other traditional democratic freedoms, have been lately admitting that Christianity may be much more important, even more *vitally necessary,* to the survival and preservation of Western Civilization than they realized. Atheist historian Tom Holland recently wrote the book *Dominion: How the Christian Revolution Remade the World*, precisely demonstrating this.

But unfortunately, a very large number of ignorant and intellectually dishonest Atheists know and care nothing of the real history and real philosophical foundations of Science, as they bluster their condescending "Atheistic Flatulence" that insults and belittles religious believers as they pretend Science, which could never have started from Atheist principles, somehow belongs to them. These, unfortunately the more common kind of Atheists, are so good at "farting with their brains" this insubstantial "Atheistic Flatulence" that they have given birth to equally unpleasant and insubstantial Secularism, which likewise rejects the Christian heritage of the West and replaces it, usually, with Atheist Relativism and/or Moral Relativism, which is ultimately rooted in the Radical Skepticism which tends to separate humans from any solid base in Reality. Secularism has now taken us to the brink of losing our Human Rights and Democratic Freedoms which depend upon Christian principles. Because Secularism rests on the

Atheist Moral Relativism which Solzhenitsyn, after living in the (genocidal) first State built on Atheist principles, noted results in "impaired thinking ability." Every later State built on Atheist principles likewise quickly becoming murderous and genocidal...

. . . This author enjoyed, on Professor Stephen Hicks' website, a cartoon in which a child in pajamas comes into his parents' bedroom and says, "Mom, Dad, there's a Moral Relativist under my bed . . ." In the next panel, a close-up of the child's terrified face, exclaiming, "*they're capable of anything . . .*" ("No more reading philosophy before bed for you, young man . . ."). Yet it is no joke. The biggest real *monsters* humanity has ever known were the Atheist Moral Relativists Stalin and Mao, each of them killing more millions of humans than Hitler's Nazis, as in their morally relative way they each did their best "to make the world a better place" by, in the USSR and China, "attempting to implement a Marxist egalitarian utopia" and "establish a Socialist State." Since Relativists "make their own truth," Socialists can easily ignore and deny the facts of Marxist genocides and millions of murders, and so the "enormous number" of Western Atheists, Marxists and Socialists Solzhenitsyn pointed out, who made sure Marxism would not get the deservedly bad reputation Nazism got, have created the current unstable and polarized political situation. Where millions of Atheists and Secularists in America and the rest of the West (who are usually also "Pro-Choice-to-Kill-Humans" ideologues who follow the Marxist precedent of legal abortion) are in ignorance blithely attempting to "make the world a better place" through Neo-Marxist Identity Politics which, bifurcating all societies with Marxist "oppressed" and "privileged/oppressor" labels, is just as inherently divisive and antagonistic as classic Marxism and cannot possibly serve the Common Good of all humanity (which must be based instead on the *Equal Human Preciousness without exception, which governments are obligated to protect*, which is part of *The Foundational Principles of Human Rights and Democracy* identified from History, Science, and Logic in this book series). Marxist (and Neo-Marxist) ideology is all rooted firmly in Atheism and Radical Skepticism which denies or radically doubts *Reality* itself, and is no substitute, of course, for the Traditional Western Values and principles which actually undergird all Human Rights and Free Democracy in the West. Yet Atheists and Secularists with their subjective Relativism which is *out of touch with objective Reality* keep trying to reshape (or "reset") the world according to Atheist Marxist principles (or the newer Neo-Marxist "Identity Politics" variant of them which produces today's "Cancel Culture." "Cancel Culture" which tries to halt and erase the Free Speech of people who disagree with the Marxist-influenced. Just like every State built on Marxist principles has had no Free Speech because Marxism cannot tolerate any Free Speech to point out objective facts which are contrary to a subjectivist Marxist's relativistic fantasy dreamworld).

Clearly, Solzhenitsyn's work of exposing the ideological and practical evils of Marxism to help end it remains unfinished – and this author's book *Pro-Life Equals Pro-Democracy*, as a kind of "Sequel" to Solzhenitsyn's *The Gulag Archipelago* (following up on what that "enormous number" of Western Marxists Solzhenitsyn warned us about have been up to since), hopes to help to truly finish Solzhenitsyn's important work. Solzhenitsyn's exposé of Marxist evil in the USSR did much to facilitate the Soviet Union's sudden demise in 1991, which only Solzhenitsyn had predicted. But the West failed to heed his warnings about how the Marxists and Marxist-influenced in the West were shaping the West for a totalitarian Marxist future through controlling the "fashionableness" of just what gets reported in Western news media and taught in Western schools and universities. Solzhenitsyn's *The Gulag Archipelago*, by exposing Soviet atrocities and how they were rooted in Marxist ideology itself (they were not Stalinist deviations) indeed made it much harder for Western Socialists to openly admire the Marxist Soviet Union as they had previously.

"But there was never any such thing as Stalinism. It was contrived by Khrushchev and his group in order to blame all the characteristic traits and principal defects of Communism on Stalin—it was a very effective move. But in reality Lenin [in faithful interpretation of Marx] had managed to give shape to all the main features before Stalin came to power."
— *Aleksandr Solzhenitsyn*

But Marx himself in his 19th Century *Communist Manifesto* foresaw that Marxism in future would *adjust and change* for new situations. And indeed, just like the (very) deadly virus that Marxism is, Marxism has "mutated" and "morphed" into new forms just as seductively tempting and insidiously deadly but harder to spot, through radically skeptical Postmodernism, developed by Marxists to protect Marxism from facts, and Western Marxism is alive and well today through Neo-Marxist Identity Politics which maintains the whole approach and character of classic Marxism by reinterpreting all of history, just as Marx did, and dividing all societies past and present into groups labelled "oppressed" and "privileged/oppressor." Ultimately in order to create enough resentment and hatred between groups to create the political instability necessary to take over and *impose* Marxist ideals upon everyone. Western Marxism is alive and well today also through Neo-Marxist "Cancel Culture" which maintains the whole approach and character of classic totalitarian Marxism by *controlling society by controlling which voices and which information gets heard.*

Marx himself knew that his Marxist utopian vision was so radical it would need to be *forced* upon people at first. Eliminating personal property and wealth in favor of State control of resources (as Socialists still seek to do) and doing away with the Traditional Family, which Marx mocked as much as some of today's Neo-Marxist Identity Politics ideologues do, as they too try to rewrite what a human family is. Without any reference to the Science of Biology, which concurs that following Traditional Western (Judeo-Christian) Sexual Values of *sex reserved for marriage* (also the universal, cross-cultural norm for sexual relations throughout history) gives the *best chance* that the next generation of human children naturally produced by the lifetime-committed married sex partners will be raised to emotionally and physically healthy human maturity in a *stable, loving human family* which is the building block of a *stable, loving human society*. But the radically skeptical Atheist Relativism inherent in all forms of Marxism has no use for facts or Science . . .

◆

CHAPTER 8
SCIENCE, MEDICINE, FREEDOM THREATENED BY *RELATIVISM NOT REALISM.*

Science Itself, Not "Just" Free Democracy, Is Now Under Threat (in Western Universities Long Compromised by Marxism as Aleksandr Solzhenitsyn — Who Knew the Signs of Marxism Better than Anyone — Repeatedly Warned the West).

Professor Jordan Peterson Rings the Alarm Bell: "The Activists are Now Stalking the Hard Scientists . . . I Have Watched The Universities Of The Western World Devour Themselves In A Myriad Of Fatal Errors Over The Last Two Decades, And Take Little Pleasure In Observing The Inevitable Unfold . . . *Research Prowess Is No Longer as Important as Willingness to Mouth The Appalling Commonplaces Of Political Correctness In The Hallowed Corridors Of Academe* . . . Wake up, [Scientists]: Your Famous Immunity To Political Concerns Will Not Protect You Against What Is Headed Your Way Fast Over The Next Five Or So Years . . ."[4]

My fellow Canadian intellectual for Free Speech, Professor Jordan Peterson's June 2020 article drawing out the significance of recent events affecting the scientific

---

[4] https://nationalpost.com/opinion/jordan-peterson-the-activists-are-now-stalking-the-hard-scientists#main-content , accessed July 5, 2020.

establishment in our country sadly demonstrates how our country (his and mine), embarrassingly, not only leads the world in Pro-Choice 'Creeping Totalitarianism' undermining Free Democracy with totalitarian laws against Free Speech, but is also leading the natural progression of the current worldwide Neo-Marxist Identity Politics ideology, which is rooted in radically skeptical philosophy, into attacks on the hard sciences themselves. His entire article is very much worth reading, but in a few brief selections below, Peterson writes:

I have watched the universities of the Western world devour themselves in a myriad of fatal errors over the last two decades, and take little pleasure in observing the inevitable unfold...

... research prowess is no longer as important as willingness to mouth the appalling commonplaces of political correctness in the hallowed corridors of academe...

... A highly cited professor of physics, who ... has garnered 100+ publications and 7000+ citations in a highly technical field ... had his standard Canadian Federal grant application rejected because he had failed to sufficiently detail his plans to ensure diversity, inclusivity and equity (DIE) practices while conducting his scientific inquiry. It is now standard practice for university hiring boards to insist that their faculty job applicants submit a DIE plan with their curriculum vitae — a terribly dangerous occurrence of its own.

I believe that the fundamental reason such plans are required, particularly of those who practice in the so-called "hard" STEM fields (science, technology, engineering and mathematics) is so that those who could not hope to assess the quality of research endeavours in those specialties as a consequence of their own inability or ignorance, can be made into judges by enforcing the adoption of standards of attitude and behaviour that have nothing to do with the fields in question...

SCIENCE, MEDICINE, FREEDOM THREATENED

... Wake up, STEM denizens: your famous immunity to political concerns will not protect you against what is headed your way fast over the next five or so years.[5]
— Dr. Jordan B. Peterson

Peterson's article details how another, highly productive chemical research scientist with a recent peer-reviewed article in one of the prime academic chemistry journals in the world *was severely punished* after a handful of Identity Politics ideologues started a Twitter Mob against him for writing something disagreeing with their vacuous and Neo-Marxist ideology. Peterson notes that shamefully the "Provost and VP Academic at that institution, saw nothing wrong with stabbing one of his university's most esteemed scientists in the back at the first sign of trouble." Instead of standing up for the integrity of the Natural Sciences, the hard sciences, the university and the world-class peer-reviewed scientific journal both unconscionably and immediately caved in to the political pressure exerted by a small number of noisy Neo-Marxist Identity Politics ideologues and punished an exceptional scientist. Here the scientific establishment shows the same craven, spineless cowardice we have gotten used to from the so-called "conservative Right" in my country, which similarly frequently fails to stand on principle even to "conserve" *The Foundational Principles of Human Rights and Democracy* against the continuous assaults of the Pro-Choice and Neo-Marxist legal human-killing abortion Extremist Left...

♦

---

[5] https://nationalpost.com/opinion/jordan-peterson-the-activists-are-now-stalking-the-hard-scientists#main-content, accessed July 5, 2020.

William Baptiste

. . . Atheism and Secularism (and the Relativism and Marxism which influences them) are ultimately religious worldviews requiring a "Leap of Faith" - and are a leap not near as reasonable to take as Christianity, since Christians developed Modern Science in the Christian universities of Christian Europe, working logically from a Christian worldview and from First Principles the West learned from the Bible. Christian Pro-Life Principles also undergird all Human Rights and Free Democracy . . .

. . . Have you heard that "all religions are equal"? This is an Atheist dogma. What it really means is that (from the Atheist perspective), all (traditional, theistic) religions are equally *wrong*; equally *irrelevant to modern life.* While their own (non-theistic, a-theistic) answer to the big First Order or "religious" questions is to believe (*in religious faith not proof*) in the non-existence of any intelligent Orderer of the universe or Creator God. Even though this leaves Atheists with no explanation for the fantastically intricate *order* in the material universe, magnificent and intricate *order* which scientists were only motivated to look for in the first place *because of their "First Principles" assumption* (coming to the ancient Greek scientists from the Jewish Bible, Christian Old Testament, and developed into Modern Science and the Modern Scientific Method by devout Christians at the Christian universities of Christian Europe) that the universe is an *intelligently ordered cosmos*, and NOT a fundamentally *random* and undirected *chaos.* In any case, only someone severely uneducated or unintelligent would ever claim "all religions are equal." All religions (including the ultimately religious philosophical position of Atheism, which believes on faith not proof in the non-existence of God) are manifestly NOT equal, above all *not equal* in *compatibility* with the *Foundational Principles of Human Rights and Democracy.* Which come from Christianity, so Christianity

SCIENCE, MEDICINE, FREEDOM THREATENED

is (by far) the religious worldview *most* consistent with Human Rights and Free Democracy (and most consistent with *Science*), while Atheism is the (ultimately religious) worldview that is among the very *least* compatible with either Human Rights, or Free Democracy, or Science. Atheist (usually Marxist) governments have proven time and time again they are among the most oppressive and murderous governments history has ever known, and logically so, since Atheist Moral Relativists can accept no human-loving God of Christianity to set any absolute standards for human behavior, nor absolute moral principles, such as *killing humans is wrong; equal human preciousness; Human Rights;* or any of the (Christian) *Foundational Principles of Human Rights and Democracy.* Also, no Atheists were involved in the founding of Modern Science because those who believe in no ordering intelligence for the universe have no motivation to search for *patterns of order* . . .

"Nothing worthy can be built on a neglect of higher meanings and on a relativistic view of concepts and culture as a whole."
"The generation now coming out of Western schools is unable to distinguish good from bad. Even those words are unacceptable. This results in impaired thinking ability."
". . . We have arrived at an intellectual chaos."
— *Aleksandr Solzhenitsyn*

♦

"Such as it is, the press has become the greatest power within the Western World, more powerful than the legislature, the executive and judiciary. One would like to ask; by whom has it been elected and to whom is it responsible?"

WILLIAM BAPTISTE

— *Aleksandr Solzhenitsyn*

Once Solzhenitsyn was out of the oppressive Soviet Union and in the "Free West," living in the U.S. for 18 years, he noticed and pointed out that the West was headed, if more slowly, in the same direction as the Marxist Soviet Union (towards totalitarianism), only by a different route. Solzhenitsyn even noticed and pointed out how the censorship of news and ideas which was essential to totalitarian Soviet Socialism and Communism just found a new, more subtle and insidious expression in the West:

"Without any censorship, in the West fashionable trends of thought and ideas are carefully separated from those which are not fashionable; nothing is forbidden, but what is not fashionable will hardly ever find its way into periodicals or books or be heard in colleges. Legally your researchers are free, but they are conditioned by the fashion of the day."
 — *Aleksandr Solzhenitsyn*

Those intellectually dishonest (or "ideologically lobotomized") Western, Soviet-sympathizing (often Atheist) intellectuals and Marxist ideologues (with "impaired thinking ability" from philosophical "relativism" Solzhenitsyn spoke of) **never left the "Free West."** Instead, still full of *denial* of all the well-established human-killing evil that has consistently come from any attempts to put Relativist Atheist Marxist Socialist ideology into practice on the State level, they became professors at Western universities teaching Westerners (as Solzhenitsyn indicated in 1983) *to hate their own society* (especially through Neo-Marxist Identity Politics) and they have since raised up generations of Western leaders who have for decades been shuffling off the trappings of Traditional Western Values and Western Christian Civilization (including the philosophical *Realism not Relativism* which grounds Science) on which Human Rights and Free Democracy were historically and logically built. Which is why this author's Prime Minister of a supposed democracy openly admires Marxist Communist China, which has no religious freedom and forced abortions; and which is why this author can now be arrested and imprisoned in my country for promoting *Equal Human Rights for All Humans* anywhere near where humans are being legally killed, following the 1920 Marxist Soviet Socialist/Communist precedent of legal human-killing by abortion.

The now "Pro-Choice Left" today have been formed by for decades witlessly imbibing ultimately anti-democratic and anti-human *extremist* Leftist ideology at Western universities, as well as there imbibing anti-scientific Postmodernist philosophy which dementedly denies any *objective facts* – Postmodernism was developed by Marxists to protect Marxism from the overwhelming *objective facts* that Marxism/ Socialism, which looks very nice on paper, is fundamentally *unrealistic* and does not work at all in practice, but always results in oppressive totalitarian States murdering millions. Thanks to the centuries-old philosophical errors ultimately resulting in today's Pro-Choice Extremist Left also having *very little grip* on *scientific, objective Reality*. Being thus "ideologically lobotomized" and *divorced from Reality* by a bad underlying philosophical worldview perhaps explains why Pro-Choicers often present themselves as so unintelligent – or so wilfully, culpably unintelligent – stupidity by *choice* – that they do not even "get" the science that preborn humans are humans and thus abortion kills humans; nor do they "get" the logic that to deny preborn humans any *Inherent Human Rights* through legal abortion is to deny ourselves any *Inherent Human Rights*, since all of us began our human existence as preborn humans. There is no way to beat the perfectly scientifically sound logical syllogism *All humans have Human Rights; Preborn humans are humans. Therefore, preborn humans have Human Rights.* But neither facts, nor science, nor logic mean anything to unthinking relativistic Pro-Choice bigots with *ideology instead of education.*

The famous journalist Malcolm Muggeridge before his death insightfully commented upon this (consciously or unconsciously) chosen philosophy yielding "imbecility," in the quotation below.

British journalist Muggeridge had himself been such a supporter of Socialism that when young he actually went to live in the Union of Soviet Socialist Republics, excited to live in the world's first Socialist State. Until while there he witnessed the Soviet *Holodomor* Genocide perpetrated in Ukraine first-hand, tried to report on it, and found himself attacked, discredited, and fired by the Western (Socialist-influenced) journalistic establishment, which actually gave the Pulitzer Prize for journalism to his fellow British (Socialist) journalist Walter Duranty, who denied and helped cover up the genocide, even though he privately admitted he knew about the millions of deaths under Soviet policies. Like the former Marxist Socialist and former Soviet Red Army captain, historian Aleksandr Solzhenitsyn (who was exiled to the West for later exposing Soviet terrors in his book *The Gulag Archipelago*), formerly Socialist Malcolm Muggeridge also saw the Marxist, Socialist corruption of Western institutions (and Science itself, according to Marxist-developed anti-scientific Postmodernism) steadily increase, such that before his death in 1990 he predicted:

SCIENCE, MEDICINE, FREEDOM THREATENED

So the final conclusion [will] surely be that whereas other civilizations have been brought down by attacks of barbarians from without, ours had the unique distinction of training its own destroyers at its own educational institutions, and then providing them with facilities for propagating their destructive ideology far and wide, all at the public expense. Thus did Western Man decide to abolish himself . . . himself blowing the trumpet that brought the walls of his own city tumbling down, and having convinced himself that he was too numerous, labored with pill and scalpel and syringe to make himself fewer. Until at last, having educated himself into imbecility, and polluted and drugged himself into stupefaction, he keeled over - - a weary, battered old brontosaurus – and became extinct.
  – *Malcolm Muggeridge*[6]

In the "drugged . . . into stupefaction" part the insightful Muggeridge correctly predicted the recent Western trend in many countries (including this author's) to legalize psychoactive drugs like marijuana, long proven to lead to even harder drug use (and there are even new movements to legalize all illegal mind-affecting drugs). Nothing could be more supportive of an eventual totalitarian takeover of the West than dulling the minds of citizens with drugs so they do not notice (or care) how their democratic freedoms are shrinking under Pro-Choice Extremist Left governments. In fact, this trend just makes it more disturbingly obvious how prophetic was Aldous Huxley's 1932 novel *Brave New World* about a dystopian future. While the USSR, the world's first Socialist State, a totalitarian State which had already legalized abortion, thus starting to control human reproduction in 1920, had already started the 1932-33 *Holodomor* Genocide killing millions of this author's ethnic

---

[6] https://www.goodreads.com/book/show/5622444-vintage-muggeridge, accessed August 25, 2020.

heritage, Huxley published a dystopian novel describing a future totalitarian world government which controlled human reproduction and kept the masses of humans distracted from realizing how *not free* they were by constant movies and entertainment, encouraging unbridled sexuality, and dulling their minds with drugs. Sound familiar? Today's West is getting closer and closer to Huxley's dystopian totalitarian vision of the future!

Journalist Malcolm Muggeridge witnessed the 1932 *Holodomor* Genocide first-hand while Huxley's prophetic book was published, and personally suffered the totalitarian censorship of the news in support of the totalitarian Soviet State not by Soviet, but by *Western* Marxists and Socialists! And, seeing the growth of Marxist thinking subverting the West ever since, before he died he wrote the West was indeed "training its own destroyers at its own educational institutions, and then providing them with facilities for propagating their destructive ideology far and wide, all at the public expense," Westerners thus "educating themselves into imbecility" — which is so easy to see now with the wide proliferation of anti-scientific Postmodernist thinking developed by Marxists like Jacques Derrida in order to protect Marxism from facts.

Having so "educated themselves into imbecility" as Muggeridge noticed; having developed such an "impaired thinking ability" from relativist philosophy as Solzhenitsyn described, today's legal-human-killing Pro-Choice Leftists do not even realize that the only reason they on the Left (including the "Liberal" media) are sometimes tempted to call outspoken people on the Right "far-Right," or even extremist "Nazis" is because their Pro-Life opponents (including U.S. President Trump who ran on a Pro-Life platform which he was consistently true to) **only look "extremely" far to the Right of them – from their vantage**

SCIENCE, MEDICINE, FREEDOM THREATENED

point firmly planted on the Pro-Choice, legal human-killing following Soviet Marxist precedent, *Extremist Left.* When the mainstream media Solzhenitsyn warned us was Marxist-influenced calls something "far right," it usually just really means more or less normal, centrist politically – since the mainstream media itself now represents and expresses the Neo-Marxist Extremist Left.

CHAPTER 9
SOME POLITICAL INSIGHTS FOLLOWING FROM THE ABOVE PHILOSOPHICAL "PENSÉES": BIFURCATED, INCOMPATIBLE UNDERLYING PHILOSOPHICAL WORLDVIEWS LEAD ULTIMATELY TO TODAY'S POLARIZED POLITICS INCLUDING THE ABORTION DEBATE (THE EQUAL HUMAN RIGHTS FOR ALL HUMANS DEBATE)

[Note: This Non-Partisan author, thinker and logician emphasizes that the Abortion Debate (the Equal Human Rights for All Humans Debate) is *not* an issue of political Left versus political Right; but an issue of political *extremism*. The killing of humans by abortion was first legalized in 1920 in *Extremist*

Left Marxist (Communist-Socialist) Soviet Russia, before this murderous Extreme Left regime also legalized and carried out the genocide of millions of born humans (legal abortion had already established the government did *not* believe *killing humans is wrong*). The killing of humans by abortion was next legalized in 1934 in *Extremist Right* Fascist Nazi Germany, this murderous Extreme Right regime also legalizing and carrying out the genocide of millions of born humans. Eleanor Roosevelt, a politician of the *real* (not extremist) Left, led the formation of the United Nations' 1948 *Universal Declaration of Human Rights*, of which there is no legitimate nor logical nor intelligent nor intellectually honest interpretation which allows for legal abortion, as abundantly demonstrated within this HUMAN RIGHTS EDUCATION FOR LASTING FREE DEMOCRACY book series.]

The Traditional Western (Judeo-Christian) Pro-Life Family Values which include and support *The Foundational Principles of Human Rights and Democracy* identified from Science, Logic, and Human Rights History in *Pro-Life Equals Pro-Democracy* are rooted in the very same philosophical stream of (Aristotelian and Scholastic/Thomist) Philosophical *Realism* as is Science, Logic and Technology — *Realism* which accepts the *objective reality* of the physical universe we humans all commonly perceive and daily interact with, and which Science studies, producing *technology* from what Science learns about *Objective Reality*.

In contrast, today's Pro-Choice, Neo-Marxist Identity Politics "Cancel Culture" and Postmodernist-influenced politicians and political parties are all rooted in the anti-scientific philosophical stream of (Cartesian and

Incompatible Worldviews; Polarized Politics

Postmodernist) Philosophical *Radical Skepticism* which denies or radically doubts there even is any knowable objective reality outside of any individual subject's own mind. An ultimately *diseased* and hypocritical view of *reality itself* which (while hypocritically staying alive by accepting reality) in philosophy and politics denies any *objective facts which might guide their politics*, leaving only *subjective feelings and opinions* and in some the deranged beliefs people can "create their own reality" and "create their own morality" (The latter as Atheist Relativist Nietzsche promoted, influencing the Nazis; the Nuremberg Trials of the Nazis were essentially the Free West's judgement for *Realism* over *Relativism* as necessary for human safety, just as *Realism* over *Relativism* is necessary for Science). Today's Pro-Choice, Neo-Marxist Identity Politics "Cancel Culture" politicians are rooted in this very same anti-scientific stream of Radical Philosophical Skepticism which (in the really existing universe) has given the world mentally deranged *solipsism* (nothing exists for sure outside your mind) and *Marxism's many tens of millions of murders (the first ten million of this author's ethnic group)* in persistent denial of the *reality* that *unrealistic* Marxist principles *do not work in the really existing world.*

(Marxists, of course, were the first group murderously deranged and divorced from reality enough to legalize human-killing abortion, in 1920, before legalizing genocide.)

"Atheist teachers in the West are bringing up a younger generation in a spirit of hatred of their own society... [they say] why should one refrain from burning hatred, whatever its basis—race, class, or ideology? Such hatred is in fact corroding many hearts today. This eager fanning of the flames of hatred is becoming the mark of today's free world. Indeed, the broader the personal freedoms are,

William Baptiste

the higher the level of prosperity or even of abundance—the more vehement, paradoxically, does this blind hatred become...
This deliberately nurtured hatred then spreads to all that is alive, to life itself...
— *Aleksandr Solzhenitsyn*

But Skeptics and Relativists (the two always go together), no matter how much they deep down doubt or deny any external objective reality exists (making the existence of anything, including moral values like "killing humans is wrong," *subjective*, and thus "relative" to each individual subject), *always find themselves still stuck in the same commonly-experienced world and universe with the rest of us, and with scientists, who accept as REAL our common human experience of the world, which even enables you, the reader, to read this book and understand it.* Regardless of Relativist notions (rooted in Skepticism that the universe we commonly perceive even really exists at all) that you can "make your own Reality" and "make your own Morality," Relativists still, just like all of us who think the world we daily interact with is *Real*, are daily confronted with the same sense data (that the sun rises in the morning and sets in the evening every day, for Relativists as much as for Realists). Skeptic and Realist alike are forced by the nature of Reality and the nature of our physical senses that put us into *contact* with it, to actually live in the Real World as it is, which Science studies to learn more about it, occasionally making discoveries which later enable clever humans to invent new technologies which can indeed transform our world and the precise way we live our lives. But technological transformations of the world only come from rigorously and logically studying its *Reality,* not from denying or doubting it. Every Skeptic and Relativist stays alive daily only by using Common Sense that assumes the world is *real*. The universe is *real*, therefore, fire and traffic and cliffs are dangerous, and we cannot "make our own reality" wherein these are not dangerous, so we must concede to the common human sensual experience of reality just to stay alive. And it is *not reasonable* skepticism, but *radical* Skepticism, even truly *demented* Skepticism, very like a mental illness which makes us incapable of living in the world and requiring medical care to keep us alive, to not trust that our senses do in fact put humans in contact with a REAL universe external to and independent of our own minds, as Science and Common Sense assume. The only way to "make your own reality" is to reject the one that daily confronts your senses and retreat into madness, insanity; and the only way to avoid a stupid death in this case is to let the medical staff (trained in the real Sciences of Medicine and Psychiatry) take care of you, since you can no longer do it yourself. Radical Skepticism and the Relativism flowing from it is not a way to live, it is a way to die.

Political change can happen in the Real World, but healthy political change can only happen if it is rooted in fundamental, philosophical *Realism* which (scientifically, and grounded in Common Sense) takes the universe of Reality as it is and works within its *real* constraints. Sophisticated but *unrealistic* Marxism which has murdered many millions has resulted from politics rooted in the philosophically Skeptical, Atheistic, Relativistic stream of "Modern Philosophy" since Descartes ...

Descartes unhinged Western Philosophy from its scientific grounding in Aristotelian and Scholastic *Realism* only inadvertently. He was a good Catholic Christian who did not foresee the damage and genocides which would result. Descartes escaped radical skepticism himself, but, since our bad ideas can take on a life of their own, he still inadvertently introduced radical Cartesian Skepticism into Western Philosophy, the "Cartesian Split" which foolishly prioritized *thought* over *existence* when Descartes erroneously stated,

"I think, *therefore* I am." Following in this philosophical stream, Skeptic German Atheist Relativist Nietzsche promoted the Relativist notion that you can "make your own morality" (a "Master Morality"), later influencing and enabling Hitler's Nazis to run Germany and make its laws from a new Moral Code which included legal racist genocide mass murders in support of a German "Master Race." **Philosophically speaking, Nuremberg later was at base a Trial of *Realism* passing official judgment over *Relativism*, because after Nazi Germany the Free World realized the *Real World* could not afford another Nazi Germany, another State run by Morally Relativistic ideology. The Nuremberg War Crimes Trials of the Nazis assumed and helped us clarify that even though all the atrocities of Nazi Germany were technically *legal*, for the future safety of all humanity, which cannot afford another Nazi Germany, any "sovereign country's" laws are still subject to certain minimal principles which even International Law must formally recognize (not create), principles we now call *Human Rights*, which were in fact formally clarified in the new United Nations' *Universal Declaration of Human Rights*, produced in 1948, while the Nuremberg Trials were still going on.** The same year the Nuremberg Trials called legal abortion in Nazi Germany a "crime against humanity" along with all the other many Nazi crimes against humanity which equally denied Equal Human Rights to some humans. **The Nuremberg War Crimes Trials established that for world human safety, the excuses "it was legal in my country" and "I was just following orders," which in most cases mitigate personal responsibility, did not, could not and must not mitigate responsibility for all the horrors in Nazi Germany that the Nazis led but in which the people participated or collaborated (or at least allowed to happen without resisting, even many otherwise good people,** which is why Professor Jordan Peterson reminds us, "the lesson of World War II: You are the Nazi." Solzhenitsyn confirms, "The battleline between good and evil runs through the heart of every man"). The Nuremberg War Crimes Trials established that these minimal political principles for governing humans we now call *Human Rights*, which are not given by any government and *so cannot be legislated away by any government*, of course imply *Human Responsibilities* to recognize those Human Rights in all other humans (and protect them where they are threatened).

Thus, the Nuremberg War Crimes Trials legitimately prosecuted key figures in Nazi Germany who led or greatly facilitated the mass murders, even though such mass murder was "legal" in Nazi Germany, because these people had *criminally neglected* their *Human Responsibilities* to recognize and protect Human Rights in other humans. Hence, not just the Nazi government leadership, but judges, doctors (especially abortionists), businessmen and others in positions of authority who particularly promoted and facilitated the Nazi crimes against humanity were put on trial at Nuremberg. Businessmen who fulfilled Nazi government contracts for customized equipment with no purpose but to kill large numbers of humans quickly, could not claim they were merely "doing business for the government" in building and supplying the Nazis with instruments of mass murder ...

CHAPTER 10
THE LOGICAL FALLACY OF *INVALID APPEAL TO AUTHORITY*. THIS IS ABOUT THE ONLY *LOGICAL FALLACY* IN A LOGIC TEXTBOOK WHICH THE PRO-CHOICE LEGAL HUMAN-KILLING ABORTION *EXTREMIST LEFT* DOES *NOT* TYPICALLY USE TO DISHONESTLY "DEFEND" LEGAL ABORTION BECAUSE THEY CANNOT FIND ANY AUTHORITY STUPID ENOUGH TO CLAIM ABORTION IS OBJECTIVELY, SCIENTIFICALLY GOOD FOR *ANY* OF THE HUMANS INVOLVED IN IT

... But the Pro-Choice Neo-Marxist Left use it to dishonestly "defend" many of their other political positions; and they use this intellectually dishonest logical fallacy to invalidly and incorrectly vilify anyone who disagrees with them as somehow "unscientific" just for having a different opinion than themselves, on topics on which there is disagreement even among qualified experts and scientists and *therefore a non-expert citing an expert who happens to agree with them does not settle the issue, since qualified experts themselves disagree.* The Marxist-influenced Western Mainstream Media which Solzhenitsyn warned the West about frequently support Western Pro-Choice, Neo-Marxist totalitarian-oriented political parties and governments in using the logical fallacy of *invalid appeal to authority* by mostly or exclusively reporting on experts who happen to agree with (or literally work for) the Marxist-influenced government, while not reporting on (and even deleting from YouTube!) experts – even large numbers of experts and scientists – who disagree with government policies – *deliberately and dishonestly creating the false notion* that "Science" somehow backs up the (Relativist, Marxist-influenced) government's policies [Update: including Coronavirus Pandemic policies], when in fact the science concerning the policy in question is not at all settled ...

. . . Unscientific, Relativist politicians and bureaucrats thus blithely make decisions affecting the very health of citizens and their precious children which *ignore or pretends solid scientific evidence against their decision does not even exist.*

[Update: This is becoming increasingly obvious in the case of long continuing oppressive government "Coronavirus" lockdowns which destroy small businesses and make people dependent upon the centralized government (which supports the centralized Marxist "Great

THE INVALID APPEAL TO AUTHORITY

Reset"); and increasingly oppressive mask-wearing etc. mandates during the now long-extended Coronavirus Pandemic, while these governments do not even consider and simply *pretend there is no* increasing number of regional, national and international doctors' and nurses' organizations against "Coronavirus alarmism" and lockdowns etc., notably the Great Barrington Declaration, drafted by world-class infectious disease epidemiologists and public health scientists, and, at time of writing signed by 13,796 and counting [2nd Printing Update: now 15,707 and counting] other medical scientists and 41,890 and counting [Update: now 46,412 and counting] doctors and other medical practitioners. The medical scientist signatures are followed up and vetted, so just which universities or medical institutes these medical scientists work for is verified. This is hugely important medical testimony any *healthy* democracy would seriously consider before ever considering current policies that drastically restrict so many normal democratic freedoms and civil liberties – and destroy the world economy *in order to make people desperate enough* to allow the Neo-Marxists to try their Relativist Marxist "Great Reset."]

Unscientific, Relativist politicians and bureaucrats thus blithely make decisions affecting the very health of citizens and their precious children which *ignore or pretends solid scientific evidence against their decision does not even exist.*

Why? *Because to skeptical philosophical Relativists*, like Pro-Choice politicians, all they need to do is *merely make the claim* that their position is superior, and not actually back it up with facts, well-established facts or otherwise, ultimately *because they do not believe in any objective facts*, but only in subjective feelings and opinions (ultimately because deep down, following the (temporary for him) radical Skepticism of Descartes, they cannot really be *certain* anyone else than themselves even *exists*, so why negotiate with or concede to others of differing opinions? Descartes himself escaped the radical consequences of the Radical Skepticism he unleashed in the world, but his bad idea still haunts and threatens Western Civilization) . . .

. . . Such Relativism is why, as this author has observed, really committed Pro-Choice ideologues may pretend to be intelligent and try to back up their position, but without any commitment to reason or logic or science or facts at all. **Genuinely intelligent and intellectually honest people, who are not "ideologically lobotomized," can be convinced by facts, reason, logic to change their position. But once a committed Pro-Choice ideologue realizes, while in argument with a knowledgeable, intelligent person such as this author and Human Rights scholar, that all the facts of Human Rights History, Science and Logic do not support their Pro-Choice position, and that all their typical arguments for legal abortion are *logical fallacies* (as demonstrated in this book series), instead of (with intellectual honesty) changing their position to Pro-Life, they suddenly retreat completely into unintelligent Relativism and claim the Abortion Debate (The Equal Human Rights for All Humans Debate) is *just a matter of subjective opinion*, such that their (uneducated and illogical) Pro-Choice opinion is just as valid as my (highly educated and logical) Pro-Life opinion**. "Well, that's true for *you*, this [contradictory position] is true for *me*." Because to Skeptics and Relativists, there is no objective truth, nor objective facts of any kind. But by so easily accepting such *contradiction* in order to save their weaker position from being proven wrong by the stronger, they actually violate and deny Aristotle's *Principle of Non-Contradiction* — which is the easiest thing in the universe to prove, the first of Aristotle's First Principles of Being, and the foundation of all Logic and Science!

CHAPTER 11
RELATIVISM IS BOTH SCIENTIFICALLY STUPID AND POLITICALLY DANGEROUS BECAUSE IT DOES NOT CHOOSE WHICH DIFFERING SUBJECTIVE OPINION SHOULD BE IMPLEMENTED IN PUBLIC POLICY BASED ON *FACTS*; BUT RATHER ONLY BASED ON *POWER*. (POWER VIA MANIPULATION; BY THREAT; OR BY VIOLENCE)

Relativists not Realists on the surface at first can seem so friendly and conciliatory, since they will not tell anyone they are *wrong,* but may rather say "that's true for you; this [contradictory thing] is true for me."

But here is where the Pro-Choice (and/or) Neo-Marxist Identity Politics ideology, rooted in Radical Skepticism and the Relativism that follows, gets really politically dangerous. Since to them there are *no objective facts, only subjective feelings and opinions,* therefore *all politics is just a matter of competing subjective opinions*; and since no facts are admissible to settle disputes between subjective differences of political opinion, how are disputes settled so public political policy can be made? The only thing Relativists recognize for this purpose is *power.* Those who have more *power*, more *force*, can get their subjective opinion of how things should be run into political practice, over all competing subjective opinions about politics. Without any objective facts from which to judge the most reasonable, the most logical, the most scientifically sound political policy, which will be most beneficial and safe for the most humans, public policies instead get decided only by *which subjective opinion* has the most *power* to *force* itself upon all other human subjects. And ever since Marxism began, if the Marxist-influenced cannot physically, violently, militarily *force* their Marxist ideology upon everyone in a country through the bloody violent revolution Marx expressly recommended, they will try to *EMOTIONALLY MANIPULATE others into making political concessions to their vacuous and unrealistic ideology*, by using the Marxist system and its categories which are explicitly designed to engender *sympathy* in others. Marx unrealistically and over-simplistically reinterpreted of all political history as one kind of "class struggle" or other between those Marxists label "oppressed" and those Marxists label "privileged/oppressor," just so Marxists can then take the side of the "oppressed" underdog against the "privileged" oppressor, generating sympathy for their

The Invalid Appeal to Authority

political cause because they have painted themselves as the "compassionate" "social justice warrior" and righter of wrongs (even very old wrongs they have dishonestly exaggerated into current hatred and division for Marxist ends. There is no reason today's "White" people here in Canada, where American Black slaves went to be free, need to "apologize" for slavery in another country in another century. Yet Neo-Marxists here in Canada have demanded we do a witch-hunt for "systemic racism" in Canada; Canada which Martin Luther King, Jr. himself said was the "heaven" the American Black slaves were singing about in the classic Negro spiritual songs (in a lecture series Dr. King delivered in Canada's capital of Ottawa). While the Neo-Marxists tear down statues and absurdly echo the American BLM call to "defund the police" (note BLM is run by *self-described Marxists*) . . . There is no sense to today's Neo-Marxist Identity Politics, and I believe most who follow it have merely been blinded by the false seductive glimmering beauty of the "Marxist egalitarian utopia" which has deceived so many before. But part of them really does like and appreciate living in a Free country. So, I believe that all that is needed is to really challenge the ideologues, as this book series does, forcing them to become consistent and *choose* just which path they will follow, and most once so challenged (as with THE INTELLECTUAL HONESTY CHALLENGE) will take the philosophically Realist path which supports Human Rights and Freedoms and rejects Relativistic Marxism in all its forms (including Pro-Choice Neo-Marxist Identity Politics with its "Cancel Culture") . . .

. . . it is sadly true that some of the more "ideologically lobotomized" with the relativistic "impaired thinking ability" Solzhenitsyn spoke of will continue to hang on to their *ideology instead of education* with its unrealistic delusions . . . And if the Pro-Choice Extremist Left cannot (yet?) physically or militarily force their Marxist-influenced ideals and opinions (and deadly practices like legal human-killing abortion) on the rest of us as did the Marxist Communist Socialists under the blood-stained Marxist despots Lenin, Stalin, Mao, Pol Pot and so on, *they resort to shouting down and trying to verbally (if not physically) slander and intimidate those with different opinions than themselves.* Hence, numerous examples like those of: [note: much more detail on these is included in *Pro-Life Equals Pro-Democracy*]

1. Pro-Choice and/or Neo-Marxist Identity Politics "Cancel Culture" ideologues surrounding Dr. Jordan Peterson's McMaster University talk with megaphone and noisily shouting him down so no one could hear him, with loud repeated vulgar insults and intimidating but absurd accusations (since they could not win an argument with someone so intelligent and honest any other way);
2. Marxist Pro-Choicers organized by the "Proletarian Feminist Front" of the "Revolutionary Communist Party" similarly noisily (and with shrill whistles) shouting down the Candlelight Prayer Vigil Service before the Canadian National March for Life, and intimidatingly standing eye-to-eye with the Pro-Lifers on the stage, literally covering up their Pro-Life signs advocating *Equal Human Rights for All Humans* (while city police who work for the Pro-Choice Mayor who facilitated the first of the laws in Canada to make peaceful Pro-Life Human Rights advocacy a crime, in the national capital run by an aggressively Pro-Choice party, just let the Revolutionary Communist Party-organized Pro-Choicers violate the democratic freedom of expression and assembly of Pro-Life Canadians who actually believe in the (Pro-Life) *Foundational Principles of Human Rights and Democracy* – not just at the Prayer Vigil, but the next day police just let the Communist-organized Pro-

The Invalid Appeal to Authority

Choicers interfere with and shorten the March for Life itself by blocking the pre-approved March route);

3. Numerous cases of Pro-Choice university students and/or administration suppressing the free expression of Pro-Life views on university campuses, even to the point of violent destruction of Pro-Life displays (while campus security is conveniently absent) and administration threatening expulsion of and revoking the official university club status of Pro-Lifers – again, because there is no way Pro-Choicers can win rational arguments with Pro-Lifers based on facts, science, logic, reason, as abundantly demonstrated in this book series; so philosophically radically skeptical and relativist (often Marxist or Neo-Marxist) Pro-Choicers, who deep down have *so little grip on reality* that they do not believe in nor can be swayed by objective facts, just threaten, intimidate, and shout down all rational discussion in order to keep their uneducated subjective opinion for Pro-Choice legal human-killing abortion legal. ***Power and force to impose your own subjective opinion on others and on public policy is all that matters when you do not believe in any objective facts because you are a skeptical Relativist.*** [Shortly before publication, this author met a group of university students who revealed another unforgivable sin of universities in my country. Not only does their university unconscionably *not allow* any Pro-Life student club which would engage in intelligent discussion and debate about the merits of the West legalizing human-killing abortion first legalized in 1920 by the totalitarian Soviet Relativist Marxists; when I asked, these *university-educated* students had *never even heard of* Aleksandr Solzhenitsyn, nor of his 35-million-copy-selling book *The Gulag Archipelago,* which exposed the facts of the Soviet Marxist Relativist evil and so helped bring down the genocidal

Marxist Socialist Soviet Union. The Marxists Solzhenitsyn warned us have infected Western Media and education have been hiding their tracks well . . .

CHAPTER 12
THE GOOD NEWS

As the Only-Seemingly-Powerful Totalitarian Relativist Marxist Soviet Union Threatening the World with Nuclear War *Fell Suddenly, Quickly, Bloodlessly* Due to Simple Things Like Solzhenitsyn Merely *Speaking the Truth* Against the Web of Lies that Sustained It; and the *Solidarity Movement* of Soviet-Bloc Citizens who, Despite All Marxist Attempts to Expunge Traditional Western Values, Still Held on to and STOOD UP TOGETHER IN SOLIDARITY FOR the Traditional Western (Judeo-Christian) Values Which Include and Support *The Foundational Principles of Human Rights and Democracy* Identified from Science, Logic, History (and the History of Ideas) in This Book Series;
SO WILL FALL SUDDENLY the Only-Seemingly-Powerful Relativist-Marxist-Influenced "Shroud of the Dark Side, Confusing Everything," Which Solzhenitsyn Warned the West had Infected Western Media and Universities, Which it has with its:
1-Radically Skeptical and Relativistic, Anti-Realistic and Anti-Scientific and Anti-Factual Postmodernist Philosophy Designed by Marxists to Protect Marxism from the *Facts* Marxism/Socialism Does Not Work in The Real World; and with
2- Neo-Marxist Identity Politics Which Unrealistically and Toxically Divides All Political Past and Present into Needlessly Adversarial and *Specifically Marxist* Categories of "Oppressed" and "Privileged," to *Create* the Current Polarized Political Instability for Marxist Ends Including Cutting Off Western Civilization from Its Own History and

from the Traditional Western Values Which Made it Great and Free; and with

3-Neo-Marxist "Cancel Culture" Which Just Like Classic Marxism Attempts to Control Society through "Cancelling" Opposing Voices - through Censorship Controlling Just Which Voices and Information Gets Heard; and with

4-Pro-Choice(-to-Kill-Humans) Ideology Following the Totalitarian Relativist Marxist Soviet 1920 Legal Abortion Precedent, Which Legally Eradicates the *Inherent Human Right to Live*, Leaving No Minimal Foundation for a Free Democracy (and Explaining the Around 100 Million Murders in Marxist Countries the Last Century Since 1920).

All These Relativist Threats to Lasting Free Democracy Will Fall Suddenly When Enough People (Embracing *Scientific Realism* Over *Skeptical Relativism*) Simply Speak the Truth Against the Web of Lies and Stand Up *Together* in *Solidarity* to Save Science, Medicine, Freedom in the GLOBAL SOLIDARITY MOVEMENT.

"Writers haven't got any rockets to blast off. We don't even trundle the most insignificant auxiliary vehicle. We haven't got any military might. So what can literature do in the face of the merciless onslaught of open violence?
One word of truth outweighs the whole world."
— *Aleksandr Solzhenitsyn*

THE GOOD NEWS

"You can resolve to live your life with integrity. Let your credo be this: Let the lie come into the world, let it even triumph. But not through me."
— *Aleksandr Solzhenitsyn*
"The simple step of a courageous individual is not to take part in the lie. One word of truth outweighs the world."
— *Aleksandr Solzhenitsyn*

Here is the really GOOD NEWS in all of this. Nobel Prize-winning author and historian of Soviet Marxism Aleksandr Solzhenitsyn with his 35 million copy-selling book *The Gulag Archipelago* exposing Marxism in practice really did send the torpedo to sink the ship of Marxism which destroyed his beloved country of Russia first by making it the world's first (philosophically *Relativist not Realist*) Socialist State, the Union of Soviet Socialist Republics (USSR), which erased human freedom and killed many tens of millions of people to establish and maintain itself (all while seeking to implement the seductively beautiful-sounding but utterly *unrealistic* and *relativistic* "Marxist Egalitarian Utopia"). Solzhenitsyn's book exposed Marxist lies and evil for all to see and exposed the roots of all that evil in (Relativistic) Marxism itself, proving it was what Marxism required to establish itself. Proving rampant totalitarianism and human-killing evil was not just an aberration or failure of Marx's followers, but a "congenital birth defect" of Marxism itself, conceived upon all the manifestly stupid and unrealistic assumptions of the relativistic stream of bad philosophy identified in this present book. After *The Gulag Archipelago* was published, all the intellectually dishonest Marxists and Socialists in the West no longer convinced themselves, and no longer tried to convince everyone else, that Marxism was wonderful and that the Soviet Union as the world's first Socialist State was to be emulated.

So, because of Solzhenitsyn simply speaking the truth against the web of lies necessary to sustain Marxism-Communism-Socialism, what we are facing today is an already wounded form of Neo-Marxism. Those Western Marxists too dishonest to admit that Marxism did not work and abandon it, dishonestly committed the "sleight of hand" my fellow Canadian intellectuals for Free Speech, Professor Jordan Peterson and Professor Stephen Hicks have called attention to, re-imagining Marxism as Postmodernism, ultimately resulting in Identity Politics which continues Marxist principles, but not so strong and violent a form. A wounded form which (like classic Marxism) only lives by lies and deceit, but no longer having the bloodlust of classic Marxism. Though they still divide all society and all history into classes labelled "oppressed" and "privileged oppressor," today's Neo-Marxists no longer relish the thought of bloody revenge upon their perceived "oppressors" (or are less likely to; prominent Pro-Life Human Rights advocates have sometimes been deluged with death-threats and "doxing" by Pro-Choice Identity Politics ideologues). But it seems the real vengeful bloodlust of classic Marxism has been made too intolerable by the tens of millions of Marxist murders in all the earlier attempts to establish a Marxist State.

So, this author believes most who today are fooled by Neo-Marxist ideology are just that – fooled. They do live in the West and enjoy its freedom. They no longer, thanks to Solzhenitsyn exposing the truth about the USSR, hold up the Marxist USSR as their Socialist ideal. If they have kept Marx's foolish and unrealistic Socialist ideals, they no longer have Marx's utter disdain for thoughts of establishing a Socialist State without violence. I think many of them really want the world to be a better place; they are not committed, as classic Marxists were, to violence as the way. They are merely not educated enough to yet understand that the Marxist principles and the Marxist utopian vision itself is dangerous (and inherently violent) because of the false, bad philosophical assumptions it is built on. So, they just need to be educated. This book series attempts to provide this HUMAN RIGHTS EDUCATION FOR LASTING FREE DEMOCRACY, and finish Solzhenitsyn's work in ending Marxism, by rooting out the Marxist infestation in the West which Solzhenitsyn's book *The Gulag Archipelago* warned us of; by showing how to build a lasting and just Free Democracy with Equal Human Rights for All Humans without all the Marxist Socialist errors intertwined, which make them foolishly speak of "Social Democracy" or "Democratic Socialism," not even realizing that that is essentially what the Marxist USSR and Cambodia thought they were doing. The Soviets sometimes called their system "Soviet Democracy" and Marxist Cambodia even called itself "Democratic Kampuchea" – and murdered one quarter of the population . . .

. . . It is important to realize that the mighty Marxist "evil empire" of the Union of Soviet Socialist Republics (USSR) itself, which first legalized abortion (eradicating in law the *Inherent Human Right to Live*); committed the first of many Marxist genocides (against this author's ethnic group); and threatened the whole world with nuclear extinction with its totalitarian Marxist ideological opposition to human freedom backed by a nuclear arsenal; *fell suddenly*, quickly and bloodlessly, against all expectations, due to simple things like Solzhenitsyn's motto, "one word of Truth outweighs the whole world." Solzhenitsyn simply spoke the Truth in opposition to the system of lies that sustained the Marxist Soviet Union. Soviet Totalitarianism ended due to simple things like people living under that oppressive totalitarian Soviet Bloc standing up together in *Solidarity* (in Soviet Bloc Poland) for the Traditional Western (Judeo-Christian) Pro-Life Family Values which include and support what this author has identified from Science, Logic, and

Human Rights History as *The Foundational Principles of Human Rights and Democracy*. We too can speak the Truth against the lies of Neo-Marxism, and against the Marxist practice of legal human-killing abortion; we too can stand up together in *Solidarity* for the Traditional Western Values Human Rights and Democracy are built on, to become once again the guiding principles for Western public policy . . . They brought down the militarily mighty but philosophically bankrupt Soviet Union by doing this. We only have to bring down the vacuous silliness of Neo-Marxist Pro-Choice bigots who (like all bigots) deny equal human worth and equal Human Rights to all humans, while only "defending" this bigoted Pro-Choice-to-Kill-Humans position by ignoring the science of the human life-cycle and committing almost every *logical fallacy* in a logic textbook, all because they are *Relativists not Realists* who do not have even a basic grip on either Science or Logic (as demonstrated thoroughly in other books in this HUMAN RIGHTS EDUCATION FOR LASTING FREE DEMOCRACY book series) . . .

. . . The Marxist-influenced do not know how to make the world a better place. Their Marxist, Relativist assumptions sabotage all their attempts. Categorizing all history and all current societies into toxic adversarial groups labelled "oppressed" and "privileged/oppressor" like Marx did just foments and encourages human strife and can never even possibly make the world a better place. But *Equal Human Rights for All Humans* based on Traditional Western Values like *equal human preciousness* can. Because these are in fact precisely the historical and logical *Foundational Principles of Human Rights and Democracy* . . .

"In actual fact our Russian experience . . . is vitally important for the West, because by some chance of history we have trodden the same path seventy or eighty years before the West. And now it is with a

The Good News

strange sensation that we look at what is happening to you; many social phenomena that happened in Russia before its collapse are being repeated. Our experience of life is of vital importance to the West, but I am not convinced that you are capable of assimilating it without having gone through it to the end yourselves. You know, one could quote here many examples: for one, a certain retreat by the older generation, yielding their intellectual leadership to the younger generation. It is against the natural order of things for those who are youngest, with the least experience of life, to have the greatest influence in directing the life of society. One can say then that this is what forms the spirit of the age, the current of public opinion, when people in authority, well known professors and scientists, are reluctant to enter into an argument even when they hold a different opinion. It is considered embarrassing to put forward one's counterarguments, lest one become involved. And so there is a certain abdication of responsibility, which is typical here where there is complete freedom....There is now a universal adulation of revolutionaries, the more so the more extreme they are! Similarly, before the revolution, we had in Russia, if not a cult of terror, then a fierce defense of terrorists. People in good positions—intellectuals, professors, liberals—spent a great deal of effort, anger, and indignation in defending terrorists."
– Aleksandr Solzhenitsyn

But there is HOPE! The solid HUMAN RIGHTS EDUCATION in *Pro-Life Equals Pro-Democracy* [and this little book] thoughtfully unravels about 380 years of bad thinking which brought us to this current critical 'tipping point' where the West can either lose or reinforce its Free Democracy. Yes, it was a tough assignment, thinking through centuries of errors to unravel them in order to make any sense of the flabbergasting present situation starting shortly before 2015 with (where I lived) the first attacks on Pro-Life (2500-year Hippocratic Medical Tradition) doctors' *Freedom of Conscience*, making me ask "why is my supposed free democracy acting more and more like a totalitarian State and barely anyone is noticing it?" (Other than Professor Jordan Peterson, living a few hours' drive away under the same regional and national governments as this author, who almost two years later became famous for calling attention to some of the many Pro-Choice-Left-led government violations of normal democratic freedoms including Free Speech). It took this author seven years of deep thinking, deep reflection on a lifetime of reading and learning (including being a professor teaching a university course covering the period in which *The Foundational Principles of Human Rights and Democracy* were laid), *thinking* as much as possible through much injury and illness (and deaths) affecting myself (and my family). But now there is Hope! This book (together with the other book manuscripts on this problem produced in the last seven years, to be published next) provides a solidly grounded HUMAN RIGHTS EDUCATION FOR LASTING FREE DEMOCRACY. Which should give the flabbergasted non-extremist political parties, for now mostly on the "conservative Right," *the confidence they now lack to challenge the Pro-Choice, legal human-killing Extremist Left* (remember, this non-partisan scholar does not vilify the Left; only *Extremists* Right or Left, like the Extremist Left Soviet Marxists and Extremist Right Nazis, who were the first two political parties to legalize human-killing abortion. This non-partisan author only calls the current totalitarian-oriented, Pro-Choice-to-Kill-Humans Extremist Left to get back to its democratic roots nearer the political Center – as when U.S. Democrat Eleanor Roosevelt of the "Real" Left led the production of the UN's *Universal Declaration of Human Rights*, which cannot be intelligently interpreted any way that allows for legal human-killing abortion, as shown in my books. Free Democracy for the long-term needs both political "progressive Left" and "conservative Right" to be in a healthy balance and *both* grounded in *The Foundational Principles of Human Rights and Democracy*, if either side has since strayed from this commitment (both sides have in different ways and degrees) – a commitment to democratic principles which was implicit when our modern democracies were first formed. This book series just makes those *implicit* foundations of Free Democracy more *explicit*, so they may be restored and more easily maintained in future, so that people and parties are not tempted to stray from them again, for the sake of human freedom that *lasts for centuries* on its firm historical and logical *foundations*.

"If you are willing to say that murder and genocide in many cultures over many decades is wrong, then Marxism is wrong."
– Professor Jordan B. Peterson

As this book series shows, the world needs *not* a global "Marxist Great Reset," with all the world's Pro-Choice Legal Human-Killing Neo-Marxist Identity Politics "Cancel Culture" Ideologues enthusiastically using the Coronavirus Pandemic as an opportunity to destroy the global economy and then "reset" it according to the Relativist Marxist ideology which in the past has consistently resulted in among the most oppressive and totalitarian governments known to human history.

The world rather needs a global "*Democracy Reboot*," reloading Western Civilization and Free Democracy's solid *foundations* in philosophical *Realism* and *The Foundational Principles of Human Rights and Democracy*!

ABOUT THE AUTHOR OF THIS HUMAN RIGHTS EDUCATION FOR LASTING FREE DEMOCRACY

(The Man and the Message)

About the Author

"William Baptiste's work is crucial." --- Dr. Andrew Bennett, Senior Fellow, Religious Freedom Institute (Washington, DC); Director, Cardus Religious Freedom Institute (Ottawa); Canada's first Ambassador of Religious Freedom, appointed by Prime Minister Stephen Harper

---

"5 out of 5 stars ... A book worth reading ... I would like to highly recommend this book ..."
— *Dr. James Harold, Professor of Philosophy (sometime Philosophy Department Chair), Franciscan University of Steubenville, in his Amazon.com review of the first printing of William Baptiste's book* **Realism Versus Relativism**

"Writers haven't got any rockets to blast off. We don't even trundle the most insignificant auxiliary vehicle. We haven't got any military might. So what can literature do in the face of the merciless onslaught of open violence?
One word of truth outweighs the whole world."
— *Aleksandr Solzhenitsyn*

"You can resolve to live your life with integrity. Let your credo be this: Let the lie come into the world, let it even triumph. But not through me."
— *Aleksandr Solzhenitsyn*

About the Author

"The simple step of a courageous individual is not to take part in the lie. One word of truth outweighs the world."
— Aleksandr Solzhenitsyn

The Voice Speaking with Intellectual Honesty and Clarity to Our Unstable Times (Where Free Democracy and Even Science Itself is Threatened) How to Build Human Rights and Democratic Freedoms to Last for Centuries on Their Firm Traditional, Historical, Philosophical, Scientific and Logical Foundations (and How to Restore the Integrity of Science and Medicine on Their Firm Foundations)

**William Baptiste: Life-Long Learner; Scholar; Logician; Political Philosopher; Ecumenist; Theologian;
Author of <u>DEMOCRACY 101</u>;
<u>Pro-Life Equals Pro-Democracy</u>;
<u>Knights of Human Rights, Ladies of Lasting Democracy (Handbook Manifesto of the Global Solidarity Movement)</u>;
<u>The Anti-Communist Manifesto</u>;
<u>Realism Versus Relativism</u>;
<u>The Foundational Principles of Human Rights and Democracy (Plus 10 Core Principles of Lasting Democracy)</u>;
Founder of (Non-Profit Educational Organization) Human Rights and Freedoms Forever! and The Intellectual Honesty Challenge;
Non-Partisan Thinker Calling All the World's Political Parties of Left and Right to Together Constitutionally Enshrine *Equal Human Preciousness* and *Equal Human Rights for All Humans* and Thus Explicitly Restore *The***

About the Author

Foundational Principles of Human Rights and Democracy If They Have Strayed from Free Democracy's Implicit Foundations;
Proclaimer of THE THINKING REVOLUTION (To Protect Human Rights, Science, Medicine, Freedom of Speech/Thought/Religion, and Free Democracy itself from All Accelerating Threats);

(and By His Own Admission, Author William Baptiste is Exceedingly Imperfect (Like Typical Humans); Like Everyone Else in One Degree or Another, William Baptiste is a Broken and Flawed Human Being Nevertheless Still Called (by Divine Love) to Make the Universe a Better and More Loving Place Because He is in It)

Like All Humans, Called to The *Universal Human Responsibility* to Recognize and Protect *Equal Human Rights* in All Other Humans, which is the Foundation of Free Human Societies and the Antidote to All Bigotry and Totalitarian Genocide,
Such as That Bigotry Behind the Legal Genocide Which Murdered Millions of Humans of William's Ethnicity, and the Legal Human-Killing Bigotry Started by *the Very Same Genocidal Murderers* - Legal Abortion -
which Still Continues to Kill Millions of Humans Today *Under Unwittingly Totalitarian-Oriented and Bigoted Pro-Choice(-to-Kill-Humans) Governments* which, Clueless that They Are Following Oppressive Totalitarian Precedent, Just Like the Genocidal Murderers Who First Legalized Abortion are Now Passing More and More Totalitarian Laws Against Free Speech in order to Keep Their Legal Human-Killing Legal, Against the Mountain of Evidence from Science, Logic, Human Rights History, and the History of Philosophy (Collected in William's Books) that *Pro-Life = Pro-Democracy and Pro-Choice = Pro-Totalitarianism.*

William Baptiste as a Human Rights Scholar Can Be Arrested and Jailed in His Country for Peaceful Human

About the Author

Rights Advocacy and for Speaking Scientific and Historical Facts Supportive of Democracy-Grounding *Equal Human Rights for All Humans*. Legal Abortion, Which Follows Totalitarian Legal Human-Killing Precedent in the First Place, Logically Requires Such Totalitarian Laws Against Free Speech, and the Ultimate End of Free Democracy, in Order to Keep Such an Inherently Anti-Human and Totalitarian Practice as Abortion Legal Long-term.

***

William Baptiste from a highly educated sense of *Living History* speaks boldly and intelligently and articulately for the voiceless and silenced victims of bigotry and its most extreme form, genocide:

William speaks for the millions of silenced victims murdered in the bigoted *Holodomor* Genocide of humans of his own Ukrainian ethnic group;

he speaks for the millions of silenced victims murdered in the bigoted *Holocaust* Genocide of humans of the Jewish ethnic group (plus disabled humans), Ukrainian and Jewish humans sharing a scholarly "Ukrainian-Jewish Encounter" as victims of history's two biggest bigoted genocides which occurred about the same time;

and he speaks for the millions of voiceless humans murdered in the Abortion Genocide of preborn humans just like every one of us at their age, which was started precisely by the *very same perpetrators of the world's two biggest genocides against the Ukrainians and Jews*, the (Marxist) Union of Soviet Socialist Republics (USSR) and Germany Under Adolf Hitler's (Fascist) National Socialist German Worker's Party (Nazi Party for short), the Soviet Marxists and Nazi Fascists being the first (extremist, totalitarian) political parties to legalize human-killing by abortion *precisely because these evil totalitarian political parties did not accept Democracy-grounding Equal Human Rights for All Humans nor the Inherent Human Right to Live*.

ABOUT THE AUTHOR

William Baptiste with fierce intelligence champions the Democratic Free Speech of *Pro-Life Human Rights Advocates* and *Real Doctors who do not kill humans*, Free Speech on behalf of Democracy-grounding *Equal Human Rights for All Humans*, against all the increasingly common totalitarian *Free Speech-ending* and *Democracy-ending* Pro-Choice laws and policies passed by ignorant Pro-CHOICE bigoted politicians worldwide who (like all bigots) CHOOSE just *which* humans they think have equal worth and rights and just *which* humans they think have no Human Rights and can be legally killed – just like the Soviet and Nazi bigots who were the first to legalize human-killing by abortion (and by euthanasia; and by genocide – all because they were evil and did not believe *killing humans is wrong*).

When judged according to the objective standards of Science and Logic – and undisputed facts of Human Rights History – the Pro-Choice position for legal abortion is revealed as not even remotely intellectually defensible, and not even remotely acceptable in a LASTING democracy, which can only last on Democracy's historic Pro-Life foundations. As Solzhenitsyn challenged the genocidal Marxist Soviet Communist Party, William Baptiste gives THE INTELLECTUAL HONESTY CHALLENGE in his HUMAN RIGHTS EDUCATION FOR LASTING FREE DEMOCRACY book series to every Pro-Choice Political Party which follows their legal human-killing abortion precedent to account for themselves before the public and repent of their totalitarian legal human-killing abortion evil – as intellectual honesty demands.

***

Before his Ph.D. studies at the Sheptytsky Institute and being a professor at Dominican University College (where he replaced Dr. Andrew Bennett, appointed Canada's *Ambassador of Religious Freedom*), William Baptiste got his Master's Degree with Honors at Franciscan University of

About the Author

Steubenville (FUS), where the Philosophy Chair testified in writing to the University President and others of

---

"his tremendous academic talent" and "considerable power of mind;"
noting
"It is very difficult to conquer certain ideas, especially in a discipline that is not one's own, and yet he did that in a seemingly easy and effortless way. He was able to master the ideas and "clothe" them in his own words with nothing lost in the translation. It is an extremely rare kind of student who can make a difficult discipline one's own in the space of a semester."

William Baptiste has since used this genius intelligence and a lifetime of reading (and haunting academic libraries, sometimes sleeping in them to the chagrin of university officials) to thoughtfully discern and lay out clearly from the tangled webs of historical details the "golden threads" woven throughout history that give us all our Human Rights and democratic freedoms (and Science!). It helped that he was professor of a university course covering the period during which what he has identified as *The Foundational Principles of Human Rights and Democracy* were laid; and covering many of the thinkers who laid them throughout the West.

At FUS, the famous Dr. Scott Hahn wrote William's work was

"outstanding," "excellent," "clear, thoughtful and thorough"

ABOUT THE AUTHOR

and the Theology Chair Dr. Alan Schreck endorsed William's educational Donum Veritatis – The Gift of Truth Ministries

---

"as an effective and important means to spread the faith and to promote Christian unity... It really is a 'gift' to the 'Internet Generation.'"

William was invited three times to the ecumenical Springtime of Faith Rome Summits (Catholic and Evangelical Christian leaders meeting with Vatican Officials) for being considered **"one of the dynamic leaders building the New Springtime of Faith."** William was the first Eastern Rite Christian to attend the Summits, as a member of the 20th Century's largest underground Church, which officially did not exist in the totalitarian (Atheist, Relativist, Marxist) Union of Soviet Socialist Republics (USSR) which committed the *Holodomor* Genocide against his ethnic group.

The Director of the Metropolitan Andrey Sheptytsky Institute of Eastern Christian Studies (MASI), the Very Reverend Stephen Wojcichowsky, confirmed that

---

"Mr. Baptiste is an exceptionally talented [doctoral] student"
and that
"the professors and staff of the Sheptytsky Institute are pleased that William has chosen to pursue this important [ecumenical doctoral] work at our Institute, which shares his ecumenical spirit and prays with him that Christ's disciples may indeed 'be one ... so that the world may believe'" (John 17:21),
adding that
"He has an indomitable determination to use his many gifts to serve God by working towards the reunification of the Church and bringing the Good News of salvation to the world ... William has infectious

About the Author

confidence in the love and power of the Holy Trinity and he manages to exude the joy of the Holy Spirit even when facing challenging difficulties."

Having taught a course in the Formal Science of Logic, as a logician William Baptiste reminds all those who would read his above Christian qualifications and be tempted to simply dismiss his books *merely on that basis* (instead of engaging with their powerful facts and logic with intellectual honesty), that to do so is to commit what the Science of Logic calls "the genetic fallacy" combined with "circular reasoning," known as "Bulverism." He writes,

---

"Intellectually dishonest, bigoted anti-Christian and Pro-Choice "Bulverism" first assumes that Christians and Pro-Lifers are wrong and then "justifies" turning off the brain and not listening to facts and logic presented by Christians and Pro-Lifers merely on the basis of the "wrongness" assumed but not proved (circular reasoning). Intellectually lazy Bulverists say things like "you only believe that because you're a Christian/Pro-Lifer," as if the origin or "genetics" of their opponents' belief justify simply dismissing their position (the genetic fallacy), without any regard to the overwhelming facts of Science, Logic, and Human Rights History (and the History of Philosophy) which support the conclusions that Pro-Life = Pro-Democracy and that Christianity, if it need not be individually embraced, must at least be respected by governments as the origin and source of the underlying Foundational Principles of Human Rights and Democracy, in any country that wants to remain a free democracy and not eventually fall to current 'Creeping Totalitarianism' now undermining Democracy from its very foundations."

ABOUT THE AUTHOR

William declares:

"No intellectually honest person can deny Western Human Rights and freedoms start with The Foundational Principles of Human Rights and Democracy identified herein (like equal human preciousness and the Inherent Human Right to Live), which Christianity introduced into the West, and only the intellectually dishonest would dismiss these books lightly and without engaging with their undisputed scientific and historical facts and sound logic. But LASTING Democracy, religious freedom, and Human Rights for all requires that in response to current 'Creeping Totalitarianism' these books start a DIALOGUE in Western nations about just how to ensure these highest of Western values last for the long-term."

***

[2022 Update:]

Since 2015 (when a doctors' group in his nation's capital asked him to speak against government regulation of the medical profession taking away doctors' freedom of conscience and taking away doctors' ability to practice genuine – Hippocratic - Medicine) William Baptiste has been thoughtfully developing the HUMAN RIGHTS EDUCATION FOR LASTING FREE DEMOCRACY book series while dealing with accidents, injuries, illnesses and deaths within his immediate family, including multiple hospitalizations of himself and his children. All while seeing his 2015 predictions coming true (in line with the great Solzhenitsyn's), of formerly "creeping" totalitarianism *rapidly accelerating* throughout the "Free West," accelerating even faster since the Coronavirus Pandemic (during which he had internal bleeding, anemia and debilitating headaches which took excessive time to diagnose and treat because of hospital lockdowns during the Pandemic). All this led him to urgently work the last seven

About the Author

years on *tools to restore and preserve Western freedom* as much as possible *within the limitations* of his and his family's health and well-being. Limits further imposed by successive tragedies of family deaths and hospitalizations and home floods in 2021 as he was publishing Advance Reader Copies of the first 6 book manuscripts in the series. The greatest of the tragedies was the unexpected sudden death of his wife and mother of his six children, thankfully after she had seen the birth of their first grandchild on her own birthday six weeks earlier. Grieving with his children while cleaning up their home after floods, still the irrepressible spiritual power backing up his honest intellect enables him to continue to champion for *Human Rights and Freedoms Forever* with his nascent NPO of that name, recalling the above-quoted Director of the Sheptytsky Institute's testimony that "William has infectious confidence in the love and power of the Holy Trinity and he manages to exude the joy of the Holy Spirit even when facing challenging difficulties" (such as previously doing his doctoral studies grossly underfunded). Recovering from his own latest hospitalization and gradually adjusting to life as a widower and single Dad, with both aches and hopes in his heart William hopes 2022 will at last see the fruit of the important (Dr. Andrew Bennett called it "crucial") intellectual work he has been doing for seven years amidst such difficulties – now that his newly available HUMAN RIGHTS EDUCATION FOR LASTING FREE DEMOCRACY book series proclaims THE THINKING REVOLUTION (to protect Human Rights, Science, Medicine, Freedom of Speech/ Thought/ Religion, and Free Democracy itself from all accelerating threats). Let the necessary *intelligent and honest societal dialogue* to ensure LASTING freedom (on firm foundations) begin! Only those who are (wittingly or unwittingly) part of these threats (or dull and dishonest dupes of them) will refuse to enter this vital and long overdue societal dialogue begun in the HUMAN RIGHTS EDUCATION FOR LASTING FREE DEMOCRACY book series.

About the Author

Human Rights and Freedoms Forever!

Up until Westbow Press's 2022 launch of <u>www.WilliamBaptiste.com</u> as his "author website" and a central place to order his books, William Baptiste's non-profit educational organization Human Rights and Freedom Forever! has mainly been himself thoughtfully reflecting and writing upon the rapid disintegration of normal democratic freedoms (and medical integrity) in his country and worldwide since 2015, in the light of his lifetime of reading, learning and teaching (often enough writing while convalescing from accident/injury, illness or health complications related to his injuries – his latest book <u>*Realism Versus Relativism*</u> was put together from previous work, and uploaded to the publisher, while William was himself recuperating in hospital not long after the sudden illness and death of his wife, the co-foundress of the "Baptiste Family Ministries" including William's Human Rights and Freedoms Forever!).

Previously in 2017 he made a short-run Advance Reader Copy of his first book *DEMOCRACY 101: A Voter's and*

ABOUT THE AUTHOR

Politician's Manual for LASTING Democracy - excerpts from which can be downloaded from the United Nations' *Office of the High Commissioner for Human Rights* website at this link:

http://www.ohchr.org/Documents/HRBodies/CCPR/GCArticle6/HumanRightsandFreedomsForever.docx

William's initial professionally published (though unedited) contribution to the long-overdue societal dialogue about Western Freedom's foundations, to finally start it properly (and possibly to end it quickly), written somewhat disjointedly due to frequent tumultuous advances of totalitarianism in his country and the world from 2018-2020, was <u>*Pro-Life Equals Pro-Democracy*</u>, published by Westbow Press in 2021, as a kind of "sequel" to Aleksandr Solzhenitsyn's *The Gulag Archipelago*. A new book to help finish Solzhenitsyn's brilliant work of exposing and helping end the philosophical errors (and naturally resulting political atrocities) of (philosophically *Relativist not Realist*) Marxism (atrocities like the first legal human-killing by abortion and by genocide) – in recognition of the first ten

About the Author

million victims of (Relativist) Marxist ideology in practice, from William's Ukrainian ethnic heritage, in the Marxist Soviet *Holodomor* Genocide (preceded by the first human victims of legal abortion in the same genocidal Socialist Soviet Union. Followed by many more tens of millions of victims of Marxist ideology – both born and preborn - killed in the Cold War Marxist Soviet Bloc and in Marxist China, Cambodia, Vietnam, North Korea and so on). Because (as shown in William's books) Marxism-Communism-Socialism is deeply rooted in philosophical *Skepticism* and *Relativism* (instead of the philosophical *Realism* which grounds Science, Logic, Technology, Human Rights and Free Democracy), those influenced by Relativist and Marxist thinking (including Pro-Choicers who follow the Marxist precedent of legal abortion) are prone to not take objective facts seriously nor honestly, but they wriggle out of admitting facts which do not fit their ideology as much as they can (Pro-Choicers typically avoid admitting obvious objective scientific facts like *preborn humans are humans* so *abortion kills humans)*, and they build their politics on *ideology* instead of *education.* William explains,

---

Solzhenitsyn wrote,

"To do evil a human being must first of all believe that what he's doing is good..." and wrote
"Ideology – that is what gives evildoing its long-sought justification and gives the evildoer the necessary steadfastness and determination. That is the social theory which helps to make his acts seem good instead of bad in his own and others' eyes... Thanks to ideology the twentieth century was fated to experience evildoing calculated on a scale in the millions."

This is why Marxists (and today's Pro-Choice Neo-Marxist "Identity Politics" ideologues, with their "Political Correctness" and "Cancel Culture") have never learned from all the tens of millions of human deaths resulting from every single attempt to implement at the State

ABOUT THE AUTHOR

level the seductively beautiful-sounding but unrealistic "Marxist egalitarian utopia where no-one owns anything and everyone is happy." Because what Solzhenitsyn called their "impaired thinking ability" coming from Relativist Marxism means they never learn that Relativistic Marxism just does not work in the Real world. They just keep trying to hammer (and sickle) the "Red Square peg" of Marxism into the "round hole" of Reality, no matter how many tens of millions of humans are killed in the repeated attempts. One quarter of Cambodia's population died under Marxist policies, but such facts make little difference to Relativists like Marxists (and Pro-Choicers) who doubt or deny objective facts and insist that everything is subjective and therefore relative. This subjectivist lack of grip on objective Reality is why Marxists (and today's Pro-Choice Neo-Marxists practicing "Political Correctness," "Identity Politics," and "Cancel Culture") are fundamentally intellectually dishonest and end up setting up political policies and systems built on a web of lies, just like the one Solzhenitsyn exposed in the world's first Relativist, Marxist, Socialist State, the totalitarian Union of Soviet Socialist Republics (USSR) which was the first State to legalize human-killing by abortion. Relativist Pro-Choicers following their example today cannot even use language honestly and scientifically, calling what scientifically-speaking are undisputedly unique fetal-age human lives mere "uterine contents" (abortion provider Planned Parenthood's term) or "tissue blobs." Pro-Choicers accuse Pro-Life Human Rights Advocate politicians of being "against a woman's right to choose" because Pro-Choicers cannot even speak honestly and scientifically about the fact they as Pro-Choicers believe in the right to CHOOSE to KILL what scientifically-speaking are unique living individual biological human organisms (just like each of us at their age) with absolutely unique human DNA utterly distinct from their parents at every age and stage of their human life-cycles (zygote to senior adult). Science and facts ultimately mean little to those influenced by Relativist and Marxist thinking, which is so dishonest (thanks to its "ideology over education") that the Soviet Marxist Holodomor Genocide killing 7-10 million humans of my ethnic group in 1932-33 was at the time covered up not only in the

About the Author

Socialist Soviet Union but also by Western (philosophically Relativist not Realist) Marxist/Socialist-influenced mainstream media, which actually gave the Pulitzer Prize to the dishonest New York Times journalist who denied the genocide, and discredited and fired the honest whistle-blower journalists who tried to expose the killing while it was happening.

So, we in the West must now realize just how long Western mainstream media has been Marxist-influenced (and Relativist-influenced). Solzhenitsyn, living in the U.S. for 18 years after he was exiled from Marxist Soviet Russia for exposing its evils in The Gulag Archipelago (published 1973), as a Nobel Prize-winning author, historian and the world's foremost authority on Soviet Marxism, confirmed that the same insidious (philosophically Relativist not Realist and therefore anti-scientific) Marxist ideology which he said "cannibalized" his beloved Russia had also infected Western education and mainstream media as well, through "an enormous number of Western intellectuals who felt a kinship and refused to see [Marxist] communism's crimes. When they no longer could do so, they tried to justify them." Solzhenitsyn (who died as recently as 2008) repeatedly warned the West this Relativist, Marxist influence in education and media was taking the West towards the same totalitarian ends as the Soviet Union, just more slowly and by a different route. Solzhenitsyn lamented,

"In actual fact our Russian experience... is vitally important for the West, because by some chance of history we have trodden the same path seventy or eighty years before the West. And now it is with a strange sensation that we look at what is happening to you; many social phenomena that happened in Russia before its collapse are being repeated. Our experience of life is of vital importance to the West, but I am not convinced that you are capable of assimilating it without having gone through it to the end yourselves..."

Seeing Solzhenitsyn's prediction starting to more dramatically come true at the end of 2020, in 2021 William

About the Author

Baptiste quickly followed up Westbow Press's 2021 publication of *Pro-Life Equals Pro-Democracy* with the self-published and unedited "Emergency First Edition/ Advance Reader Copy" of his new book

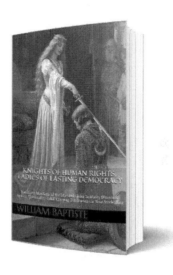

KNIGHTS OF HUMAN RIGHTS, LADIES OF LASTING DEMOCRACY
Handbook Manifesto of the [Educated] *Global Solidarity Movement* [Against Uneducated Global 'Creeping Totalitarianism' Now *Accelerating*]

as a handbook to quickly educate and equip freedom lovers everywhere to effectively stand up *together* in *Global Solidarity* for democracy-grounding (and philosophically *Realist* not *Relativist*) Traditional Western Pro-Life Family Values in public policy. So they can learn to be like the good Poles who stood together in *Solidarity* against the oppressive totalitarian Relativist Marxist ideology which had enslaved Poland, thus undermining hardline Soviet Marxist Communism in the Soviet Bloc and helping to bloodlessly end the totalitarian Soviet Union (and with it end

About the Author

the Cold War). Instead of being like the good Germans who *lost their democracy to totalitarianism* because they allowed themselves to be intimidated into *silence* and *separation* by their totalitarian-oriented National Socialist (in German, *Nazi* for short) ruling political party which (like too many Western political parties today) did not believe in *Equal Human Rights for All Humans* (hence the genocidal totalitarian, politically extremist-Right Nazi Party was the next political party after the genocidal totalitarian, politically extremist-Left Soviet Marxist Communist Party, to legalize human-killing by abortion and by genocide. The Nazis being the first to add *legal euthanasia* – today also copied by *Relativist not Realist* politicians - to their legal human-killing list). William dedicated this book

---

To my soon-coming first grandchild
I wrote this book so you, and everyone else's grandchildren, have the best chance of growing up with uncompromised democratic freedoms in countries which recognize Equal Human Rights for All Humans without any bigoted exceptions

---

ABOUT THE AUTHOR

This baby (Jacqueline) was born 6 weeks before her grandmother's sudden death, on her grandmother's birthday, with her grandmother present (William came and did baby's first photo shoot the following week). But this book (and series) is not just for her. In order to save Human Rights and democratic freedoms for everyone's children and grandchildren against all current and future threats to Free Democracy, William Baptiste has clearly articulated Democracy's implicit foundations embedded in Traditional Western Values, making them into explicit **Foundational Principles of Human Rights and Democracy**, plus **10 Core Principles of Lasting Democracy**, which can be constitutionally enshrined in Western nations to give Human Rights and freedoms a secure foundation for centuries. At this critical 'tipping point' between totalitarianism and democracy starting even before the Coronavirus Pandemic brought us even closer to losing human freedom, William Baptiste declared THE THINKING REVOLUTION for the first time in print in _Pro-Life Equals Pro-Democracy_ and in the shorter follow-up books _Knights of Human Rights, Ladies of Lasting Democracy_ and _The Anti-Communist Manifesto_.

About the Author

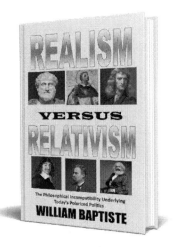

Perceiving the need to make this vital HUMAN RIGHTS EDUCATION FOR LASTING FREE DEMOCRACY even more accessible and easier to spread in even shorter, smaller books, by the end of 2021 (and in the midst of the above-mentioned 2021 successive family tragedies), William Baptiste put together (from previously published and unpublished material) two short, small books. <u>Realism Versus Relativism</u>, written last but perhaps best read first, to

ABOUT THE AUTHOR

clear away the unsound, unscientific, illogical and intellectually dishonest thinking that drives so much of today's politics. And <u>*The Foundational Principles of Human Rights and Democracy (Plus 10 Core Principles of Lasting Democracy)*</u>. The latter focuses on and highlights in a short form (ideal for giving to your elected representatives who need to know these) the positive and *practical* principles on which lasting human freedom must be based; principles developed or presented in the longer, earlier books.

All of the above books of the HUMAN RIGHTS EDUCATION FOR LASTING FREE DEMOCRACY book series (separately and together) promote a THINKING REVOLUTION and launch a *Global Solidarity Movement* for the key Traditional Western Values (and philosophical worldview) which Democracy (and Science!) were built on to be the continued guide of public policy, a movement which can rally under the Flag of Democracy William designed for the purpose, which states the necessary starting point right on the flag:

Foundational Principle of Democracy #1: Every human life, without exception, is SUPREMELY and EQUALLY precious.
Foundational Principle of Democracy #2: Every human life must be free from government coercion in matters of belief, so they may freely seek and find this beautiful truth foundational to democracy.

ABOUT THE AUTHOR

Any politician or political party that thinks they know any different and better principles (and philosophical worldview) on which to build lasting human freedom and Human Rights (and Science!) must take THE INTELLECTUAL HONESTY CHALLENGE in the books, to see if they can possibly make an intelligent and honest case for another way (good luck with that).

All those who want to be on the right side of History; the right side of Science; the right side of Logic and Intellectual Honesty; who want their children and grandchildren to live free lives, who therefore probably want to *do what they can* to help support and spread this HUMAN RIGHTS EDUCATION FOR LASTING FREE DEMOCRACY (poetically-speaking, becoming "Knights of Human Rights, Ladies of Lasting Democracy"), can contact *Human Rights and Freedoms Forever!* to order the books, flags and promotional materials, donate, volunteer (become local "Volunteer Democracy Leaders" in your area!), or book William Baptiste as a speaker for your (in-person or online) human-life-and-freedom-loving event!

About the Author

OUR WEAPON IS EDUCATION. THEIR WEAPON IS IGNORANCE.

www.WilliamBaptiste.com

Send all enquiries to
donate@WilliamBaptisteHumanRightsAndFreedomsForever.com
or Call
(613)761-0147

OUR WEAPON IS EDUCATION. THEIR WEAPON IS IGNORANCE.

YOU CAN HELP!

YOU CAN HELP FREE DEMOCRACY LAST FOREVER! CONTACT, DONATION AND VOLUNTEER SUPPORT INFORMATION

to Assist Human Rights and Freedoms Forever! with the Further Development and Distribution of William Baptiste's HUMAN RIGHTS EDUCATION FOR LASTING FREE DEMOCRACY Book Series (DEMOCRACY 101; PRO-LIFE EQUALS PRO-DEMOCRACY; KILLING HUMANS IS WRONG; NO FRUIT WITHOUT ROOTS; EQUAL HUMAN RIGHTS FOR ALL HUMANS; THINKING REVOLUTION: THE INTELLECTUAL HONESTY CHALLENGE; REALISM VERSUS RELATIVISM; KNIGHTS OF HUMAN RIGHTS, LADIES OF LASTING DEMOCRACY; THE ANTI-COMMUNIST MANIFESTO and Other Print/Audio/Video Works in Support of LASTING Human Rights, Religious Freedom, and Democracy Itself Worldwide . . .

YOU CAN HELP!

William Baptiste's New Non-Profit Educational Organization *Human Rights and Freedoms Forever!* needs your assistance in further developing and distributing William Baptiste's books and other educational resources; in having them translated, and in making educational audio and video resources based on this content. Plus promotional materials to equip "Knights of Human Rights and Ladies of Lasting Democracy" for the great task of spreading a solid *Human Rights Education* to make sure Human Rights, Religious Freedom, and Free Democracy itself survives the current attacks of 'Creeping Totalitarianism' and then thrives for centuries, secure on Democracy's historical and logical foundations in Traditional Western Values.

YOU can participate in this Democracy-preserving task by becoming a Volunteer Democracy Leader in your city or by becoming a Patron of *Human Rights and Freedoms Forever!*

To save Free Democracy; Free Speech; Freedom of Thought/Belief/Religion and *Equal Human Rights for All Humans* from all threats;
and to make current threats to human life and freedom – and to Science, which depends on *objectivity* and *Realism not Relativism* – unthinkable to start again in the future, by replacing *ideology* with *education*;
and to firmly establish the world's free nations on Democracy's (and Science's) secure foundations for centuries;
the HUMAN RIGHTS EDUCATION FOR LASTING FREE DEMOCRACY book series has distilled from the academic disciplines of History, Science, Logic and Philosophy:
The Foundational Principles of Human Rights and Democracy
(which need to be constitutionally enshrined in any democracy which wants to remain one);
Ten Core Principles of Lasting Democracy
(Practical Guidelines for setting up democracies that last for centuries on firm foundations);
The Pledge of Allegiance to Democracy;
and the Flag of Democracy as a symbol

YOU Can Help!

of what this author now calls the (educated) *Global Solidarity Movement*
against (uneducated) global 'Creeping Totalitarianism'
which is no longer just 'creeping' but *accelerating* – but only because up until now too few have had a solid
HUMAN RIGHTS EDUCATION FOR LASTING FREE DEMOCRACY.
OUR WEAPON IS EDUCATION. THEIR WEAPON IS IGNORANCE.

GET AND SPREAD A HUMAN RIGHTS EDUCATION FOR LASTING FREE DEMOCRACY
HUMAN RIGHTS SCHOLAR WILLIAM BAPTISTE CALLS FOR A *GLOBAL SOLIDARITY MOVEMENT* OF WORLD CITIZENS OPPOSING TOTALITARIAN *IDEOLOGIES* WITH HUMAN RIGHTS *EDUCATION*
All are invited to participate in this important Democracy-preserving task by *learning and spreading* the newly available HUMAN RIGHTS EDUCATION FOR LASTING FREE DEMOCRACY
Or by becoming a Volunteer Democracy Leader in your city or by becoming a Patron of the author's Non-Profit Educational Organization
Human Rights and Freedoms Forever!

You Can Help!

www.WilliamBaptiste.com

To become a "Volunteer Democracy Leader" in your city, e-mail VOLUNTEER@WilliamBaptisteHumanRightsAndFreedomsForever.com

To Become a Patron or for more donation options than those on the website, e-mail
DONATE@WilliamBaptisteHumanRightsAndFreedomsForever.com

To book William Baptiste as a speaker for your Human Rights and Freedom-loving event, e-mail
BOOKINGS@WilliamBaptisteHumanRightsAndFreedomsForever.com

To Pre-Order or to express interest in buying (or making!) Flags of Democracy, posters, bumper stickers, T-shirts or other materials to promote a HUMAN RIGHTS EDUCATION FOR LASTING FREE DEMOCRACY, e-mail
DemocracyStore@WilliamBaptisteHumanRightsAndFreedomsForever.com

Hostile readers who disagree with this book's conclusions can take THE INTELLECTUAL HONESTY CHALLENGE in this book series to see if they can make an intelligent case for remaining Pro-Choice – and concede that *Pro-Life = Pro-Democracy* if they cannot: e-mail

HonestyChallenge@WilliamBaptisteHumanRightsAndFreedomsForever.com

For more information, e-mail
INFO@WilliamBaptisteHumanRightsAndFreedomsForever.com
Telephone: 1 (613) 761-0147

YOU CAN HELP!

WilliamBaptiste.com

PayPal.Me/WilliamBaptisteHRAFF

HUMAN RIGHTS EDUCATION for LASTING FREE DEMOCRACY

Send the books to your elected representatives and leaders; to civil servants, judges, journalists, police, military; to influential 'Big Tech' Billionaires, 'Big Media' moguls, 'Big Pharma' executives *and tell them they no longer have any excuse* to not know and not support *The Foundational Principles of Human Rights and Democracy* (and the *Core Principles of Lasting Democracy*)

Manufactured by Amazon.ca
Bolton, ON